ServiceDesk Plus 8.x Essentials

A kick-start guide to implement and administer IT
Service Management processes with ServiceDesk Plus

Ankush Agarwal

BIRMINGHAM - MUMBAI

ServiceDesk Plus 8.x Essential

First published: August 2013

Production Reference: 1200813

Published by Packt Publishing Ltd.
Livery Place
35 Livery Street
Birmingham B3 2PB, UK.

ISBN 978-1-84969-664-7

www.packtpub.com

Cover Image by Abhishek Pandey (abhishek.pandey1210@gmail.com)

Credits

Author
Ankush Agarwal

Reviewer
James Gander

Acquisition Editor
Vinay Argekar

Commissioning Editor
Manasi Pandire

Technical Editor
Akashdeep Kundu

Project Coordinator
Amigya Khurana

Proofreader
Judith Bill

Indexers
Monica Ajmera Mehta

Tejal Soni

Graphics
Disha Haria

Production Coordinator
Pooja Chiplunkar

Cover Work
Pooja Chiplunkar

About the Author

Ankush Agarwal has been working in the IT Service Management domain, as well as conducting internal organization training, for more than eight years. He likes writing about service technologies and processes and has also won blogging awards in this space. He has been involved in setting up and managing various service desk teams and is currently associated with a top-tier Investment Bank.

I wish to personally thank my teams, seniors, and managers throughout my career who always trusted me with critical responsibilities during both tough and not-so-tough times. Their belief and support has helped me learn the fine details of the otherwise complicated process flows and service architectures. The on-the-job experience has also helped me relate with practical challenges and contributed in making this book more realistic and closer to the people on the ground.

I would also like to thank my wife and two-year-old son, who had to cope with my diverted attention and sacrificed late nights and weekends. I am keeping this short, to make it up to them.

About the Reviewer

James Gander, the Director of Gander Service Management Ltd, is an ITIL accredited Service Manager with over 10 years experience in managing, mentoring, and leading IT support teams in the UK, India, and New Zealand, across Outsource, Utilities, Media and Broadcast, Public Health, and Tertiary Education environments. He consults and advises Service Desks and IT Operations support teams, enabling continuous improvement whilst also delivering a stable operational environment.

James is also an accomplished people manager, varying from small local teams to large multinational teams and is experienced in strategic thinking to drive improvements and change.

www.PacktPub.com

Support files, eBooks, discount offers and more

You might want to visit www.PacktPub.com for support files and downloads related to your book.

Did you know that Packt offers eBook versions of every book published, with PDF and ePub files available? You can upgrade to the eBook version at www.PacktPub.com and as a print book customer, you are entitled to a discount on the eBook copy. Get in touch with us at service@packtpub.com for more details.

At www.PacktPub.com, you can also read a collection of free technical articles, sign up for a range of free newsletters and receive exclusive discounts and offers on Packt books and eBooks.

http://PacktLib.PacktPub.com

Do you need instant solutions to your IT questions? PacktLib is Packt's online digital book library. Here, you can access, read and search across Packt's entire library of books.

Why Subscribe?

- Fully searchable across every book published by Packt
- Copy and paste, print and bookmark content
- On demand and accessible via web browser

Free Access for Packt account holders

If you have an account with Packt at www.PacktPub.com, you can use this to access PacktLib today and view nine entirely free books. Simply use your login credentials for immediate access.

Table of Contents

Preface

ManageEngine's ServiceDesk Plus is a web-based help desk and Asset Management software program used to manage, monitor, and maintain IT assets and services in an organization. The software uses ITIL terminologies and framework and focuses majorly on Asset Management and IT request tracking.

ServiceDesk Plus 8.x Essentials is a mini handbook for Admins, Managers, and staffs involved in providing IT services to users/customers. The objective of the book is to help readers to set up and use these IT services effectively within the ITSM context. The concepts are explained using the trusted ITIL® framework, to also assist in a better understanding of ITIL methodology, while using the ServiceDesk Plus software.

What this book covers

Chapter 1, Conceptualizing IT Service Management, serves as a platform to provide a common understanding of the basic ITSM concepts and clarify the fine differences between frequently misinterpreted terms.

Chapter 2, Managing Incidents and Problems, introduces the purpose, objective, and scope of Incident and Problem Management (IPM) and will help the reader in setting up the process activities and interfaces for having a standard IPM process in their team/division/organization.

Chapter 3, Managing Assets and Configuration, explains the objective and scope of IT assets and Configuration Management and will help the reader in discovering and managing IT assets, as well as managing the software and hardware inventory and handling purchase and contractual agreements.

Chapter 4, Controlling Changes and Releases, explains the purpose, objective, and scope of Change Management and Release Management and will establish their connection with the IPM Process, and also cites the different types of changes and the framework used to effectively manage each of them.

Chapter 5, Service Desk – Where the Value Is Realized, explains why the Help Desk lies at the core of Service Management and how this function can be used to control critical processes.

Chapter 6, Making Life Easier – Handy Features, covers the miscellaneous features in the tool to aid in the day-to-day tasks.

What you need for this book

- ServiceDesk Plus 8.*x* Enterprise Edition
- A compatible browser (Internet Explorer 6, Firefox 3.6, or Google Chrome being the minimum versions)

Who this book is for

This book is for all:

- IT Help Desk Managers looking forward to optimize and streamline IT Support Operations
- IT Help Desk Administrators responsible for managing service levels by efficiently managing requests and IT Support Staff
- IT Support Staff looking to use ServiceDesk Plus features while gaining a better understanding of the ITIL framework

Conventions

In this book, you will find a number of styles of text that distinguish between different kinds of information. Here are some examples of these styles, and an explanation of their meaning.

Database table names, folder names, filenames, file extensions, pathnames, dummy URLs, user input, and Twitter handles are shown as follows: "In case of failures, `FailedCIList.csv` file could be used from the **Imported Result** page to correct the errors and resubmit, in order to avoid duplicates."

New terms and **important words** are shown in bold. Words that you see on the screen, in menus or dialog boxes for example, appear in the text like this: "The incident could also be logged from the **Quick Actions** dropdown and selecting **Create new | Incident**."

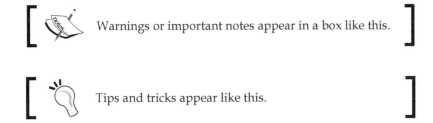

[Warnings or important notes appear in a box like this.]

[Tips and tricks appear like this.]

Reader feedback

Feedback from our readers is always welcome. Let us know what you think about this book—what you liked or may have disliked. Reader feedback is important for us to develop titles that you really get the most out of.

To send us general feedback, simply send an e-mail to feedback@packtpub.com, and mention the book title via the subject of your message.

If there is a topic that you have expertise in and you are interested in either writing or contributing to a book, see our author guide on www.packtpub.com/authors.

Customer support

Now that you are the proud owner of a Packt book, we have a number of things to help you to get the most from your purchase.

Errata

Although we have taken every care to ensure the accuracy of our content, mistakes do happen. If you find a mistake in one of our books—maybe a mistake in the text or the code—we would be grateful if you would report this to us. By doing so, you can save other readers from frustration and help us improve subsequent versions of this book. If you find any errata, please report them by visiting http://www.packtpub.com/submit-errata, selecting your book, clicking on the **errata submission form** link, and entering the details of your errata. Once your errata are verified, your submission will be accepted and the errata will be uploaded on our website, or added to any list of existing errata, under the Errata section of that title. Any existing errata can be viewed by selecting your title from http://www.packtpub.com/support.

Piracy

Piracy of copyright material on the Internet is an ongoing problem across all media. At Packt, we take the protection of our copyright and licenses very seriously. If you come across any illegal copies of our works, in any form, on the Internet, please provide us with the location address or website name immediately so that we can pursue a remedy.

Please contact us at copyright@packtpub.com with a link to the suspected pirated material.

We appreciate your help in protecting our authors, and our ability to bring you valuable content.

Questions

You can contact us at questions@packtpub.com if you are having a problem with any aspect of the book, and we will do our best to address it.

1
Conceptualizing IT Service Management

This first chapter is intended to focus on certain **ITIL** concepts while clarifying the differences between some of frequently misinterpreted terms.

Before imparting on the journey to understand how ServiceDesk Plus helps in managing IT services, let's have a common understanding of some terminologies which are commonly used but often misinterpreted. Terms such as Problem Management, Release Management, SLA, IT Process, and so, have now moved from the geek dictionary to common IT lingo. While this outspread has helped Service Management gain more focus and acceptance, it has also established the need for having a clear definition of such terms.

ITIL® has successfully provided a platform for this. The Information Technology Infrastructure Library (ITIL) is a set of practices for IT Service Management (ITSM) that focuses on aligning IT services with the needs of business. It is a practical approach for planning and delivering IT services to the business and also provides a common ground for various IT service-related terms. ITIL, being the most widely adopted approach, also provides the framework for many of the IT Service Management software and tools. ServiceDesk Plus is a popular example of such software, which helps to comprehensively manage IT assets and services.

In the following chapters, we'll see how to best manage ITIL based processes and services using ServiceDesk Plus. However, to make the best use of this book, which elaborates the services of the ServiceDesk Plus software, it is imperative to first understand some of the IT service concepts.

Please note that all terms used in this book are as defined in the official ITIL publications.

Understanding IT Service Management (ITSM)

The success of ITSM lies in putting the customer first. ITSM suggests designing all processes to provide *value to customers* by facilitating the outcomes they want, without the ownership of specific costs and risks. This quality service is provided through a set of the organization's own resources and capabilities.

The capabilities of an IT service organization generally lie with its people, process, or technology. While people and technology could be found in the market, the organizational processes need to be defined, developed, and often customized within the organization. The processes mature with the organization, and hence need to be given extra focus. Release Management, Incident Management, and so on, are some of the commonly heard ITSM processes.

It's easy to confuse these with functions, which as per ITIL, has a different meaning associated with it. Many of us do not associate different meanings for many similar terms. Here are some examples:

- Incident Management versus Problem Management (See *Chapter 2, Managing Incidents and Problems*)
- Change Management versus Release Management (See *Chapter 4, Controlling Changes and Releases*)
- Service Level Agreement (SLA) versus Operational Level Agreement (OLA)
- Service Portfolio versus Service Catalog

This book will strive to bring out the fine differences between such terms, as and when we formally introduce them. This should make the concepts clear while avoiding any confusion.

So, let us first see the difference between a process and a function.

Differentiating between process and function

A process is simply a structured set of activity designed to accomplish a specific objective. It takes one or more defined inputs and turns them into defined outputs.

Characteristics

A process is measurable, aimed at specific results, delivers primary results to a customer, and responds to specific triggers. Whereas, a function is a team or a group of people and the tools they use to carry out the processes.

Hence, while Release Management, Incident Management, and so on are processes, The IT Service Desk is a function, which might be responsible for carrying out these processes. Luckily, ServiceDesk Plus provides features for managing both processes and functions.

Differentiating between Service Level Agreement (SLA) and Operational Level Agreement (OLA)

Service Level Agreement, or SLA, is a widely used term and often has some misconceptions attached to it. Contrary to popular belief, SLA is *not* necessarily a legal contract, but should be written in simple language, which can be understood by all parties without any ambiguity. An SLA is simply an agreement between a service provider and the customer(s) and documents the service targets and responsibilities of all parties. There are three types of SLAs defined in ITIL:

- **Service Based SLA**: All customers get the same deal for a specific service
- **Customer Based SLA**: A customer gets the same deal for all services
- **Multilevel SLA**: This involves a combination of corporate level, service level, and customer level SLAs.

An Operational Level Agreement, or OLA, on the other hand, is the agreement between the service provider and another part of the same organization. An OLA is generally a prerequisite to help meet the SLA. There might be legal contracts between the service provider and some external suppliers as well, to help meet the SLA(s). These third-party legal contracts are called **Underpinning Contracts**.

As must be evident, management and monitoring of these agreements is of utmost importance for the service organization. Here is how to create SLA records easily and track them in ServiceDesk Plus:

1. Agree SLA with the customers.
2. Go to **Admin** tab.
3. Click on **Service Level Agreements** in the **Helpdesk** block.

4. **All SLA-based mail escalations** are enabled by default. These can be disabled by clicking on the **Disable Escalation** button.
5. Four SLAs are set by default—**High SLA**, **Medium SLA**, **Normal SLA**, and **Low SLA**. More could be added, if needed.
6. Click on any **SLA Name** to view/edit its details.
7. SLAs for sites, if any, can be configured by the site admin from the **Service Level Agreement for** combo box.
8. **SLA Rules** block, below **SLA details**, is used for setting the rules and criteria for the SLA.

Once agreed with the customers, configuring SLAs in the tool is pretty easy and straightforward. Escalations are taken care of automatically, as per the defined rules. To monitor the SLAs for a continuous focus on customer satisfaction, several **Flash Reports** are available under the **Reports** tab, for use on the fly.

Differentiating between Service Portfolio and Service Catalog

This is another example of terms often used interchangeably. However, ITIL clarifies that the Service Catalog lists only *live* IT services but Service Portfolio is a bigger set including services in the pipeline and retired services as well. Service Catalog contains information about two types of IT services:

- Customer-facing services (referred to as **Business Service Category**) and
- Supporting services, with the complexities hidden from the business (referred to as **IT Service Category**)

ServiceDesk Plus plays a vital role in managing the ways in which these services are exposed to users. The software provides a simple and effective interface to browse through the services and monitor their status. Users can also request for availing these services from within the module.

The Service Catalog can also be accessed from the **Admin** tab, by clicking on **Service Catalog** under the **Helpdesk** block. The page lists the configured service categories and can be used to **Add Service Category**, **Manage** the service items, and **Add Service** under each category.

Deleting a Service Category

Deletion of an existing Service Category should be done with care. Here are the steps:

1. Select **Service Categories** from **Manage** dropdown.
2. A window with **Service Categories List** will open.
3. Select the check box next to the Service Category to be deleted and then press the **Delete** button on the interface.
4. A confirmation box will appear and on confirmation, the Service Category will be processed for deletion.

If the concerned Service Category is in use by a module, then it will be grayed out and the category will be unavailable for further usage. To bring it back into usage, click on the edit icon next to the category name and uncheck the box for **Service not for further usage** in the new window.

The following two options under the **Manage** dropdown provide additional features for the customization of service request forms:

- **Additional Fields**: This can be used to capture additional details about the service apart from the predefined fields
- **Service Level Agreements**: This can be used to configure Service Based SLAs

Summary

We now understand the ITSM concepts, the fine differences between some of the terms, and also why software like ServiceDesk Plus is modeled after ITIL framework. We've also seen how SLAs and Service Catalog could be configured and tracked using ServiceDesk Plus. Let's begin our journey with understanding Incident and Problem Management.

2
Managing Incidents and Problems

Unless we are living in a perfect world, disruptions will happen. Successful teams expect this and plan to deal with them proactively. A process, therefore, should be established to manage these disruptions and to avoid them, at early stages and not as an afterthought. This makes Incident and Problem Management critical for any customer-focused organization. Once we have working Incident and Problem Management processes, there will be fewer breaches in SLAs, resulting in more satisfied customers.

This chapter covers the purpose, objective, and scope of Incident and Problem Management (IPM) and will help the reader in setting up the process activities and interfaces for having a standard IPM process in their team, division, or organization. The topics covered in this chapter are:

- Purpose, objective, and scope of Incident and Problem Management (IPM) processes
- Prerequisites
- Process flow
- Roles and responsibilities of the service desk in IPM processes
- Risks and metrics to evaluate the success of IPM processes

Although Incident Management and Problem Management are separate processes, they are logically related and have a continuous feedback system for each other's benefit. They both often use the same tools and the same guidelines for categorization and assigning priorities and hence will be discussed together.

The execution of the Incident Management process traditionally lies with the helpdesk and with the availability of an effective tool, the helpdesk could bring down the resolution time and decrease the number of recurring incidents significantly. Since many of the service requests are about recurring issues, another benefit of having a working Problem Management process is the ease in providing additional value-added services to the customer.

Understanding the purpose, objective, and scope of Incident and Problem Management

So, why are Incident Management and Problem Management different processes? Are all service requests incidents? Is a planned downtime within the scope of Incident Management? We shall answer these questions before proceeding.

Understanding Incident Management

An incident is defined as any unplanned interruption to an IT Service or reduction in the quality of an IT Service. Failure of a configuration item that has not yet impacted service is also an incident. Hence, any planned downtime will *not* be qualified as an incident, but failure of a disk from a mirror set, which might not have impacted service yet, will be an incident. Incident Management, therefore, is the process for dealing with all incidents.

The primary goal of the Incident Management process is to restore normal service operation (as defined to be within SLA limits) as quickly as possible and to minimize the adverse impact on business operations, thus ensuring that the best possible levels of service quality and availability are maintained.

The Incident Management scope includes any event which disrupts, or could disrupt, a service. These events might be brought to notice through direct calls by the users, alerts from the event monitoring system, helpdesk staff, technical staff, and more. However, this does not mean that all calls from users or all alerts from the monitoring system are incidents. Many, or rather, most of them are informational and not a potential risk to service disruption.

Incident Management, being so valuable in not only improving the availability of systems, but also in identifying other potential areas needing attention, is often one of the initial processes implemented in IT Service Management projects.

Understanding Problem Management

While the Incident Management process is focused on restoring normal operation as quickly as possible, Problem Management is focused on the underlying cause of the issue. A problem is the cause of one or more incidents. Sometimes, if an easy workaround is present to resolve the incident, the underlying cause is not given enough attention, resulting in the incident becoming recurring in nature. Problem Management fulfills this need for a separate but equally important process to prevent problems and resulting incidents from happening, to eliminate recurring incidents, and to minimize the impact of incidents that cannot be prevented.

Problem Management scope includes the activities required to diagnose the root cause of incidents and to determine the resolutions to those problems. The process also sees through that these resolutions are implemented (via Change and Release Management processes). Problem Management is responsible for maintaining all the information about the problems, workarounds, and resolutions, and to ensure that the organization is able to reduce the number and impact of service disruptions.

Problem Management itself consists of two major processes:

- **Reactive Problem Management**: This process is executed as part of Service Operations and could be managed using tools and software such as ServiceDesk Plus.

- **Proactive Problem Management**: This process is initiated in Service Operations, but is generally driven as part of the Continuous Service Improvement. It involves identifying trends aided by data, and reports around Incidents and Problems. Such reports could be easily made available from ServiceDesk Plus.

Stipulating the requirements for Incident and Problem Management

It's recommended that certain things need to be in place before setting up the Incident and Problem Management processes. These are:

- **Clear definition of service requests and incidents**: The process and all functions should be clear about what constitutes as a service request and what incidents are. The definitions should be agreed upon before proceeding to the next steps.

- **Escalation paths**: Functional and hierarchical escalation paths must be defined.

- **Categories**: A comprehensive list of categories should be identified and listed for the incidents to be classified into. The categorization proves to be very useful at later stages in identifying the areas of improvement and establishing trends during Problem Management.

- **RACI**: Responsibilities and accountability of teams and people should be clearly stated. Similarly, the list of teams or people to be consulted and/or informed for certain events should be stated.

- **Configuration Management**: Having a working and reliable Configuration Management Database (CMDB) is extremely helpful for marking incidents against Configuration Items (CI) and to find the areas needing more attention.

- **Relationship with control processes and a core system**: Flow of information from the Incident Management system to control processes (Change and Release Management) should be defined. Incident and Problem Management are very tool-oriented processes. While service desk staff might be using various tools and applications to search for solutions, there's a requirement for a core system to help manage the entire life cycle of the Incident and Problem Management processes.

  It has been widely experienced, that having the same software manage the Incident, Problem, Change, and Release increases the efficiency of the processes. A general flow between these is as follows:

  > Incident → Problem → Request for change (RFC) → Release → Problem Closed

- **Metrics**: Finally, to assess the performance of the processes and for Continuous Service Improvement (CSI), critical success factors (CSF), and Key Performance Indicators (KPIs) should be predefined.

Understanding the IPM process flow

Now that we understand the prerequisites for setting up the Incident and Problem Management processes, we can move to the process flows required to implement them.

Implementing the Incident Management process flow

A typical incident flow is shown here. Let's see how ServiceDesk Plus makes managing these critical processes easy and effective, in the following diagram:

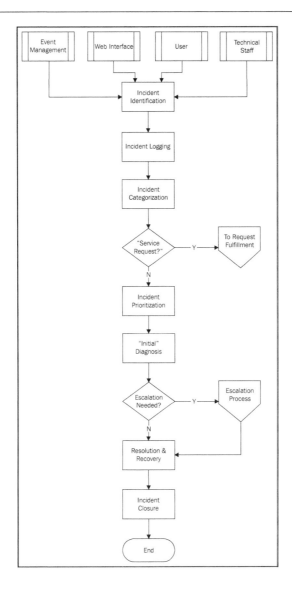

Step 1 – identifying and logging incidents

The notification of an incident could be received from:

- Event Management
- Web interface
- User, via phone call, e-mail, and so on
- Technical staff

The incident could be quickly logged into the system from the ServiceDesk Plus homepage itself using any of the following methods:

1. Using the **Quick Create - New Incident** section.

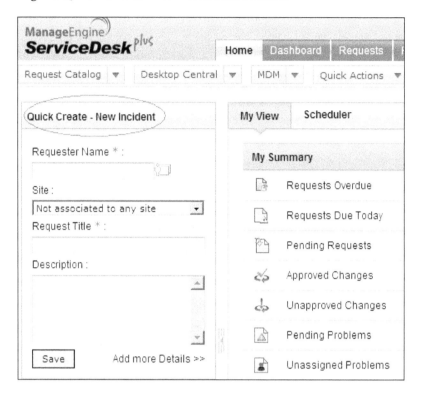

The **Quick Create** section could be enabled or disabled from:
Admin | Self-Service Portal Settings | Quick Create Settings.
Then select the radio button **Yes** or **No**, and **Save**.

2. The incident could also be logged from the **Requests** tab, by clicking on the **New Incident** button.

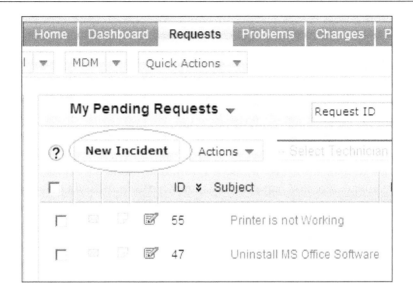

3. The incident could also be logged from the **Quick Actions** dropdown and selecting **Create new | Incident**.

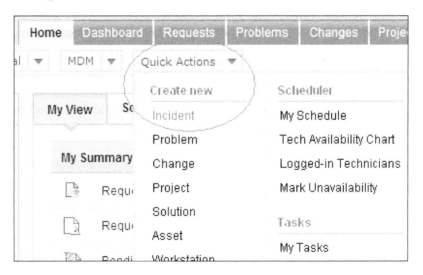

Incident templates could be created from **Admin | Incident Templates** and these templates could be used while creating new incidents. To change the template in the **New Incident** window, please select the required template from the **Change Template** dropdown.

Step 2 – categorizing incidents

Classification of incidents into categories is important in order to identify the areas of improvement and to establish trends which could be useful for other processes such as Problem Management and Supplier Management. A multilevel categorization is generally used and ServiceDesk Plus offers three levels of categorization: **Category**, **Subcategory**, and **Item**. Depending on the type of failure, incidents are assigned to these categories and the ticket could then be automatically routed to the appropriate support group.

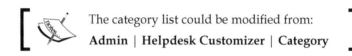 The category list could be modified from:
Admin | Helpdesk Customizer | Category

The automatic dispatch of incidents is a very useful feature offered in ServiceDesk Plus, especially when the service desk has to deal with many incidents in a day. Business rules can be created to automate the assignment of incidents to teams, categories, or levels.

The rule can be set from **Admin | Helpdesk | Business Rules | Add New Business Rule** at the top right of the the **Business Rules List** block. The rule can then be configured as shown in the following screenshot:

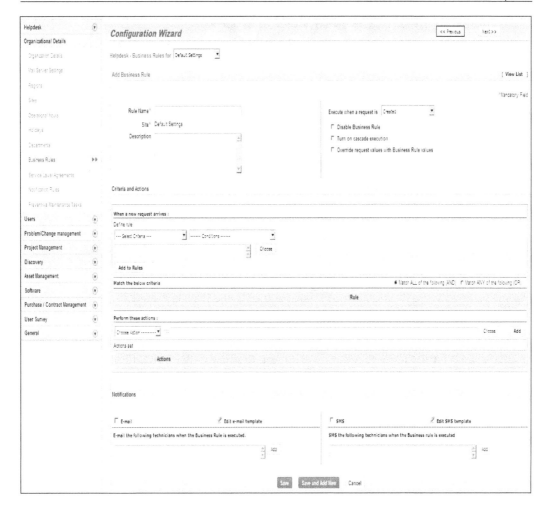

Step 3 – prioritizing incidents

Prioritization helps in estimating how quickly the business needs resolution and the impact the incident is causing. Hence, the incident priority should be determined, taking both urgency and impact into account. Very often, an Urgency and Impact matrix is defined in order to assess the priority and associated target resolution time.

 ServiceDesk Plus provides a feature to define this in the tool itself:

Admin | Helpdesk Customizer | Priority Matrix

Here's how the matrix looks, in the following screenshot:

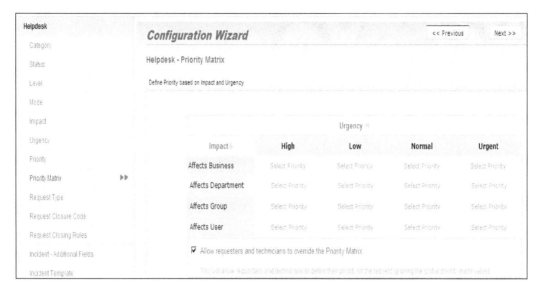

If the checkbox for **Allow requesters and technicians to override the Priority Matrix** is checked, dynamic prioritization is allowed, that is, the technician can manually assign the priority. Otherwise, only the predefined prioritization is used and the priority field in the new incident window is disabled.

 The **Impact List** could be modified or configured from:
Admin | Helpdesk Customizer | Impact

Step 4 – diagnosing incidents

The service desk must perform some initial diagnosis to discover the full symptoms of the incident and then attempt to resolve it, taking help from the **Known Error database** (KEDB). The identified workarounds or solutions can be documented or found under the **Solutions** tab.

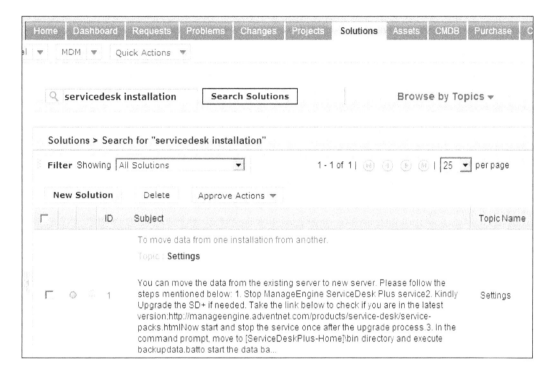

Step 5 – escalating incidents

The incident needs to be escalated as soon as it is clear that the first level of support is unable to resolve it *or* when the target time for first-point resolution is exceeded. Further escalations also need to be done on a similar basis. This is called **Functional escalation**. Certain types of incidents will also need to be escalated up the management chain; this is called **Hierarchical escalation**. However, it is to be noted that the service desk continues to own the incident at all times and is responsible for closing it. The SLAs guide these escalation processes and the notifications can be automated using the SLA rules, as also seen in *Chapter 1, Conceptualizing IT Service Management*. Here is the screenshot of the **SLA Rules** section:

SLA Rules

When a new request arrives :

○ Match ALL of the following (AND)   ⦿ Match ANY of the following (OR)

Criteria

[--- Select Criteria --- ▾] is [   ]   [Choose]   [**Add to Rules**]

Rules Set

		Rule
☒	✎	Priority is "High"

Any request matching the above rules should be responded within : 0 Days [0 ▾] Hours [10 ▾] Minutes

Any request matching the above rules should be resolved within : 0 Days [1 ▾] Hours [0 ▾] Minutes

☐ Should be resolved/responded irrespective of operational hours.
   ☐ Should be resolved/responded irrespective of Holidays.
   ☐ Should be resolved/responded irrespective of Weekends.

If response time is elapsed then escalate:

☐ Enable Level 1 Escalation

If resolution time is elapsed then escalate:

☐ Enable Level 1 Escalation
☐ Enable Level 2 Escalation
☐ Enable Level 3 Escalation
☐ Enable Level 4 Escalation

Step 6 – resolving and recovering from the incident

Actions taken to repair the root cause of an incident are termed **resolution**. Many times, when the full resolution is either not available or it is not feasible to implement it, steps are identified to minimize the impact of the incident. These steps are called **workarounds**. The resolution and workarounds are documented and are part of the **knowledge base**.

Once a workaround or a resolution is identified, applied, and the service is confirmed as fully recovered, the incident needs to be marked as resolved, and the resolution added to the knowledge base, if not already present. This could be done by clicking on the **New Solution** button from the **Solutions** tab, shown in *Step 4 – diagnosing incidents*.

Step 7 – closing the incident

Once the users agree that the incident can be closed, or after a defined and agreed period, the incident needs to be closed. The following should be considered before closing the incident:

- **Closure Categorization**: Confirm the initial incident categorization and update, if needed. The mandatory categorization fields can be configured as shown in the following information box.

- **User Satisfaction Survey**: A survey to capture user feedback. This is covered in detail in *Chapter 6, Making Life Easier – Handy Features*.

- **Incident documentation**: Complete any outstanding details thereby ensuring completeness of the incident record.

- **Need for a problem record**: Determine, in conjunction with the resolver group, technical staff, and Problem Management, if the root cause is unknown and if the incident can reoccur. If the answer is yes, then raising a problem record could be considered at this point of time.

The mandatory fields for closing a request, user acknowledgement settings, and automated closing can be configured from **Admin | Helpdesk Customizer | Request Closing Rules**. See the following screenshot:

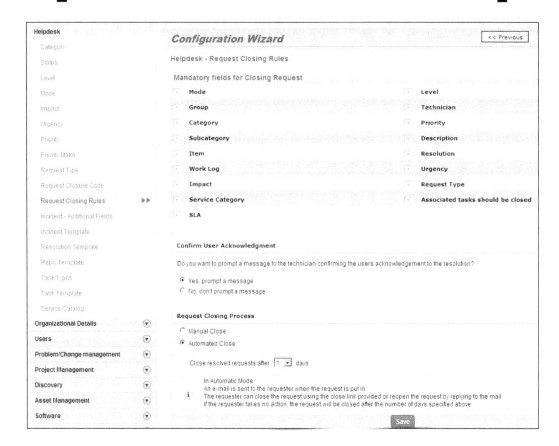

Implementing the Problem Management process flow

A typical problem flow is shown in the following diagram. Let's see how ServiceDesk Plus makes managing these critical processes easy and effective:

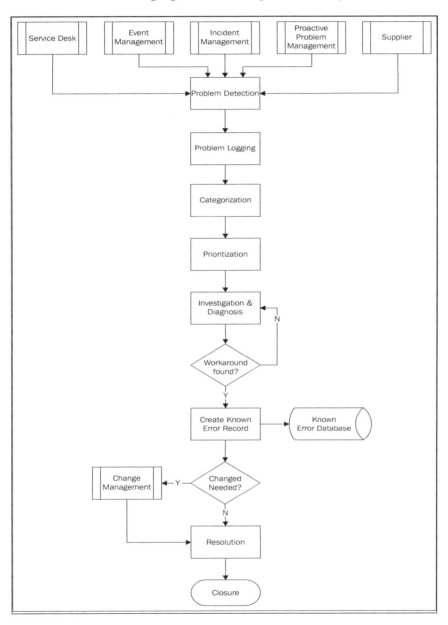

Step 1 – detecting the problem

Problems can be detected using a proactive approach (for example, through trend analysis), or through service desk records, through alerts from the event management systems, through supplier notifications, or through the incident records. Item-based reports or other similar reports can be generated from ServiceDesk Plus to identify the trend or problem areas. A regular reporting of items in the top list of incidents is generally a good indicator of a problem area.

 The reports can be scheduled in ServiceDesk Plus from **Reports | New Schedule Report**. Following is a screenshot for the **Schedule Report** window:

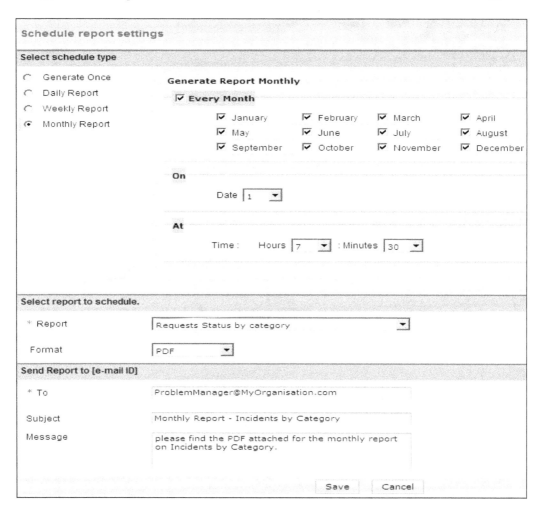

Step 2 – logging the problem

All relevant information needs to be captured in a problem record with cross-references to incidents. Care should be taken to avoid duplicate problem records for similar issues.

To associate an incident with a problem (existing or new), the steps are as follows:

1. Click on the incident subject from the **Requests** tab.
2. Click on **Search Problems** from the **Actions** drop-down menu.

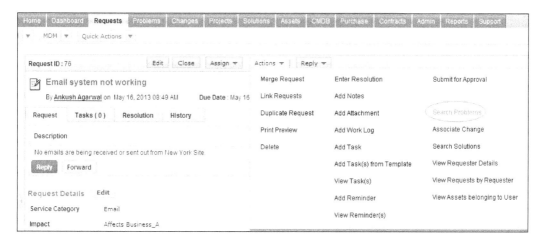

3. Filter the problems as required and associate with the one matching the requirements by selecting the radio button against it and clicking on **Associate**, or click on **New Problem**, if no problem record matching the criteria already exists.

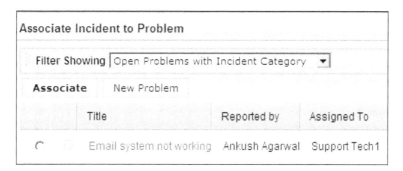

4. In case of a new problem, review and fill the details in the new window and click on the **Save** button.

Once the problem is associated with an incident, the **View Problem** and **Detach from Problem** options appear under the **Actions** dropdown.

A **New Problem** could also be logged from the **Quick Actions** dropdown or from the **Problems** tab.

Step 3 – categorizing the problem

Problem categorization is done in the same way (and often, using the same criteria) as incidents. This allows easy tracing of the problems and useful reports for the management team. As most of the problems are categorized using the same coding system as incidents, ServiceDesk Plus assigns the same categories to a problem by default, saving repeated effort. The steps to categorize are the same as the ones previously discussed in *Step 2 – categorizing incidents*.

Step 4 – prioritizing the problem

Similar to problem categorization, prioritization also uses the same coding system as incidents. However, the frequency of incidents, impacted service assets, and associated SLAs also play a major part in assessing the urgency, impact, and hence the priority of the problem. The steps are similar to the ones discussed in *Step 3 – prioritizing incidents*.

Step 5 – investigating and diagnosing the problem

Once the appropriate resources and expertize have been allocated, various techniques are used to investigate and diagnose the root cause of the incident. The Configuration Management System (CMS) and the Known Error database (KEDB) can be referred to for problem matching and for identifying the point of failure. For cases where the resolution is yet not found, the problem record must be kept open, but the workaround must be documented for temporary resolutions and a Known Error must be recorded for future reference. It is also useful to announce the problem to the users concerned, technical and management teams, to avoid duplicate incidents and to trigger faster response.

In ServiceDesk Plus, the various tabs within the **Problem** record can be used to document the analysis, workaround, and/or resolution for the problem:

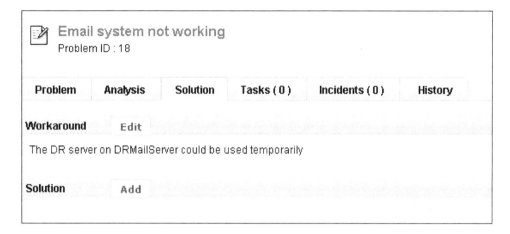

The **Make an announcement** option under the **Actions** drop-down can be used for broadcasting or e-mailing the problem details.

Notes, **Reminders**, **Tasks**, and **Work Log** can be added to the problem from the **Add New** dropdown.

Step 6 – resolving and closing the problem

Once a permanent resolution is established, it should be applied as soon as practically possible. If this involves a change in the functionality of the system, it must be applied following the Change Management process. There might be cases where an informed decision is taken to *not* implement the resolution and to live with the workaround (for example, cases where the resolution involves a higher cost than the impact does). Such cases must accordingly be documented accordingly, with the workaround readily available to the users and the service desk for faster resolution of future incidents.

After the resolution is applied and successfully reviewed, the associated Known Error records are updated, associated incidents are closed with details, and finally the problem record itself is closed , after all the relevant details have been added.

Changes can be associated with the problem record using the **Search Changes** option under the **Actions** drop-down.

ServiceDesk Plus allows us to customize the problem-closing rules as per our specific needs. This can be done from **Admin | Helpdesk Customizer | Problem/Change management | Problem Closure Rules**, as shown in the following screenshot:

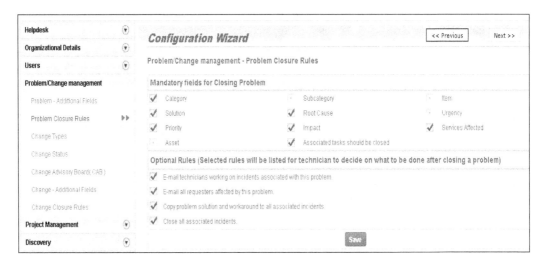

Establishing the roles and responsibilities of ServiceDesk Plus

ServiceDesk Plus is the link between the users and the IT organization, and hence is often assigned most of the responsibilities in the Incident and Problem Management process flows. However, sometimes there can be dedicated functions or teams for these. Even in such cases, certain responsibilities still ideally lie with the service desk team, such as the following:

- Incident logging
- Initial diagnostics
- Escalations at the right time
- Incident or problem record ownership (that is, updating or closing the records at the right junctures)
- User communication
- Indication of passing of Incident or Problem Management to respective functions

Assessing risks and identifying metrics

It's a good idea to be aware of the risks and to have a mitigation plan ready before adapting to the Incident and Problem Management processes:

- Lacking management and staff commitment in adhering to the process
- Non-availability of resources and tools
- Absence of prerequisites (for example, Problem Management cannot function if the Incident Management process is not followed)
- Unclear responsibilities and accountability
- Absence of technical or functional knowledge
- Inadequate training
- Resistance to change

It is also useful to establish the critical success factors for these processes and the associated KPIs. Following is just a guideline with some frequently used metrics for these processes:

- **Number of incidents or problems**: Total, per category, per priority level, reopened, repeated, escalated, and so on
- **Resolution Time**: Average, Within/Missing SLA, and so on
- Number of Incidents per known problem
- Timing of particular incidents
- Number of problems deemed uneconomical to resolve
- Number of workarounds identified, and so on

 There are many reports already configured in ServiceDesk Plus that can be used from the **Reports** tab, and more could be configured, as shown previously.

Summary

We are now ready to set up and utilize an effective and efficient Incident and Problem Management process, with mitigated risks and a focused view on continuous service improvement through various metrics and reports. We also understand the roles and responsibilities of the service desk and the detailed process flow, and how it could be implemented in ServiceDesk Plus.

In the next chapter, we will discuss how to manage IT assets, maintain the Configuration Management Database, and handle purchase orders and contracts using ServiceDesk Plus.

3
Managing Assets and Configuration

So far we've talked about managing service catalogues, SLAs, incidents, and problems. However, all processes depend on the underlying assets, and managing these assets is vital for any successful organization. This becomes even more critical for a growing organization where assets are frequently added and the relationships keeps getting more and more intertwined and complex. As we have already seen, having a view on this relationship is also needed for assessing the extent of the impact of any incident.

This chapter starts with the objective and scope of IT assets and configuration management and will help the reader in discovering and managing IT assets. The chapter will also help readers to manage the software and hardware inventory and handle purchase and contractual agreements.

The topics covered in this chapter are:

- Purpose, objective, and scope of IT Service Asset and Configuration Management (SACM)
- Managing assets via Configuration Management Database (CMDB)
- Asset Management and Definitive Media Library (DML)
- Purchase Order and Contract Management

ServiceDesk Plus provides a simple way of implementing the Configuration Management Database (CMDB) and hence managing the entire IT infrastructure. It also has a highly useful feature of asset discovery to automatically update the assets within the network. It also offers features for Vendor Management using Purchase Order tracking, Contract Management, and audit reports. We'll see the details in the following pages.

Understanding the purpose, objective, and scope of IT Service Asset and Configuration Management (SACM)

The whole purpose of having a defined process for managing service assets and configuration is to identify, control, record, report, audit, and verify all IT assets, their attributes, and their relationships. This enables other ITSM processes to be effective and also protects the integrity of the IT infrastructure. The SACM process helps define and control the components of services and infrastructure and maintain accurate configuration information on not only the current state of the services and infrastructure, but also gives a view of historical and planned states. The SACM covers service assets across the service life cycle and provides a complete inventory of assets. Any external asset or service providers which need to be controlled could also be managed using the SACM process.

It helps the business and other processes by providing complete details for:

- **Change control**: For example, forecasting, planning, traceability, and impact of changes
- **IPM processes**: For example, information on SLAs, categories, impact, root cause, and so on
- Standards, Auditory, Legal, and Regulatory obligations
- Costs of a service

Managing assets via Configuration Management Database (CMDB)

Any asset or component that needs to be managed and controlled from an ITSM perspective is called a **Configuration Item** (**CI**). It could be hardware, software, documents, and even people. The characteristics describing a CI are called its **Attributes**, and the link, dependency, or connection between CIs are called its **Relationships**.

The first step of Configuration Management is to establish a logical model of the infrastructure by recording the relationships between these CIs. This logical model is often used as the single common representation of assets and their relationships, and is used by all parts of the organization, including non-IT divisions.

The supporting system to manage the service assets and their configurations is termed the **Configuration Management System** (**CMS**). It holds all the information for the CIs in scope. The physical database used to store this information is called the **Configuration Management Database** (**CMDB**).

ServiceDesk Plus provides a simple interface to CMDB and also generates a visualization map to easily trace the relationships and interdependencies between CIs. It also supports hierarchical relationships between CIs. The tool also integrates the IPM processes and the Change Management processes within this CMDB.

Here are the steps to populate and use CMDB in ServiceDesk Plus:

Step 1 – deciding and configuring CI Types

Before starting to populate the CIs in the tool, a decision is to be made on the types and level of detail that need to be captured and controlled. While, not capturing enough information could render the CMDB futile, having too many levels of detail could also make it unnecessarily complex and ineffective. Hence, a fine balance needs to be achieved and the same enforced via the tool.

This could be done by preconfiguring the CI Types and relationships:

1. Go to **Admin | Configuration Item Types** under the **Asset Management** block.

     CI Types is the uppermost level in the CI structure.

2. Click on **Add New CI Type**.
3. Give the **CI Type Name**, **Description**, and **Save**.

4. Change the **Icon**, if needed, in the **Edit Configuration Item Type** page.

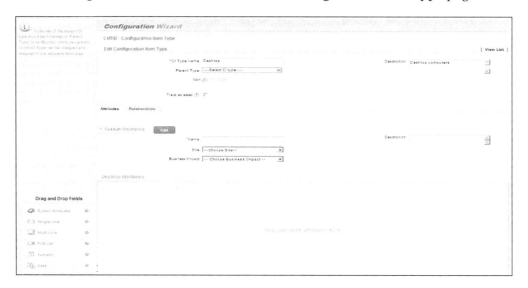

5. If the CI is also an asset and needs to be tracked under the Assets module as well, then check the **Track as asset** checkbox.

 The **Track as asset** option is available only for the parent CI Type.

6. Setting the **Attributes**:

    1. A CI can have two types of Attributes: Default and CI specific. **Default Attributes** are common to all CI types.

    2. Click on the **Edit** button to add default attributes.

    3. Any CI-specific attributes can be added using the **Drag and drop attributes here** field. These fields are customizable and offer various types for various requirements.

7. Setting the **Relationships**:

    1. Default relationships can be added from the **Relationships** tab by clicking on the **Add** button.

    2. New relationship types can be added by clicking on the **Add New Relationship Type** button from **Admin | Relationship Types** under the **Asset Management** block.

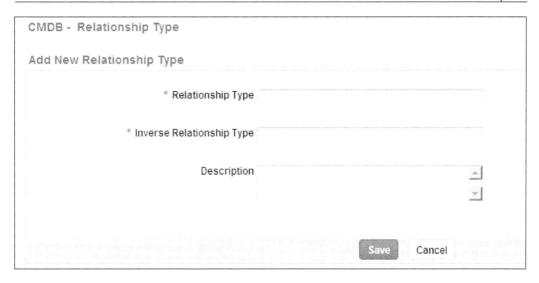

 The icon next to the CI types in the default relationships tab can be used anytime to view the complete **Relationship Map** for that CI Type. This is a very useful feature and will be discussed in more detail in *Step 3 – Creating the Information Model.*

Step 2 – populating CIs

Once the CI framework is ready, the CIs can be populated. ServiceDesk Plus offers several methods for doing so and each method is advantageous to be used for some particular types of CIs.

Method 1 – using a CSV file

If the CIs are present in a `.csv` file, the same could be imported to ServiceDesk Plus:

1. Go to the **CMDB** tab.

2. Click on the link **Import CIs from CSV file**.

3. Choose the relevant **CI Type**, locate the file, and **Submit** to upload.

 In case of failures, `FailedCIList.csv` file could be used from the **Imported Result** page to correct the errors and resubmit, in order to avoid duplicates.

Method 2 – adding new CIs manually

1. Go to the **CMDB** Tab.

2. Choose the **relevant** CI Type from the left hand pane.

3. Click on the **New** button.

4. Fill the details and **Save**.

Method 3 – Windows Domain Scan

1. Go to **Admin | Windows Domain Scan** from under the **Discovery** block. This opens the **Domain List** page with the list of all domains or workgroups discovered by the server.

2. Click on **Add New Domain** link, to add new or undiscovered domains or workgroups or

   Click on the Edit Domain icon and save the details.

3. Click on the Scan Domain icon .

4. Select the organizational units.

5. Click on **Start Scanning**.

Method 4 – Network Scan

Go to **Admin | Network Scan** from under the **Discovery** block. The rest is similar to the Windows domain scan shown in the earlier step.

Method 5 – importing from the Active Directory

Go to **Admin | Active Directory** from under the **Users** block. **Active Directory Authentication** and **"Pass-through" Authentication** can also be configured from this page.

Click on the **Import Requestors from Active Directory** link to start importing the requestors.

Step 3 – creating the Information Model

To complete the Information Model, all relationships between the CIs need to be captured. These relationships make CMDB so powerful, useful, and different from just being an Assets database.

We've seen the configuration of these relationships under step 7 of *Step 1 – Deciding and configuring CI Types*. The Relationship Map feature comes in very handy to view relationships, quickly create new ones, edit or delete existing ones, and also to view pending requests, problems, and changes for the CIs.

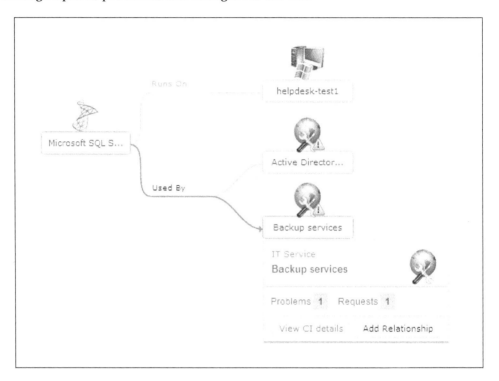

Managing Software Assets

While most of the CI management is taken care of via the CMDB, there are certain aspects of assets, for example, licensing of software, tracking of the use of certain applications (known as **Software Metering**), and so on, which need to be focused on exclusively.

ServiceDesk Plus helps to manage these aspects under various categories of Asset Management:

- **IT Assets**: These include all IP-based assets, other than workstations
- **Non-IT Assets**: These include non-IP-Based assets, such as furniture, telephones, and so on

- **Asset Components**: For example, keyboards, monitors, and even consumable components such as print cartridges
- **Software**
- **Groups**: Assets based on certain properties fall under this category

A new **Asset** can be quickly created from the **Quick Actions** dropdown:

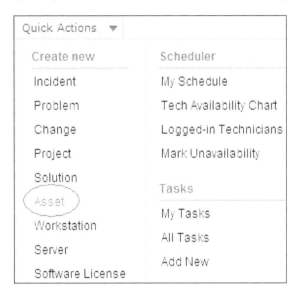

Another very useful feature available in this module is the **Remote Control**. This allows all of the scanned workstations to be reached and controlled from within ServiceDesk Plus. The steps are as follows:

1. Go to **Assets | Workstation** under the **IT Assets** block.
2. Click on the workstation name that we need to connect.
3. Select **Windows Remote Desktop** from the **Remote Control** dropdown from the **Tasks** bar at the top.

ServiceDesk Plus also helps in accurate financial reporting of assets via the Depreciation feature and can be configured at either product level or individual asset level.

 Asset-level depreciation overrides product-level depreciation.

Product-level depreciation can be configured as follows:

1. Navigate to **Admin | Product** under the **Asset Management** block.

2. **Click on the Product Name** and **choose from the Depreciation Method** dropdown. Or select all the products that have a common depreciation requirement and click on **Configure Depreciation**.

Asset-level depreciation could be configured as follows:

1. Go to **Assets**.

2. Select any asset from the left hand **Assets** pane.

3. Select the checkbox next to the asset name.

4. Click or hover on the **Actions** dropdown.

5. Select **Configure Depreciation**.

6. Choose the **Depreciation Method**, fill the details, and **Save**.

 To make quick copies of existing assets, **Copy <Asset Name>** option can be chosen from the **Actions** dropdown on the asset details page.

Tracking software and licenses

The location in which the authorized versions of all software CIs are stored is termed the **Definitive Media Library** (**DML**). The DML often also contains the associated CIs, such as the licenses and the documentations for those media. If the media is physically unavailable, the DML stores the details for downloading it. While this feature is unavailable in the current 8.*x* version of ServiceDesk Plus, it does allow the management of the software, licenses, and service packs.

The **Software** section within the **Assets** pane, on the left side, has options to achieve this:

While scanning workstations, installed software is also scanned and the details can be found under the **Scanned Software** section. This section can be used to easily track the DML details easily, including licensing-related information.

The Software Summary section is a graphical representation of most of the information in easy-to-understand graphs and summaries, as shown in the following screenshot:

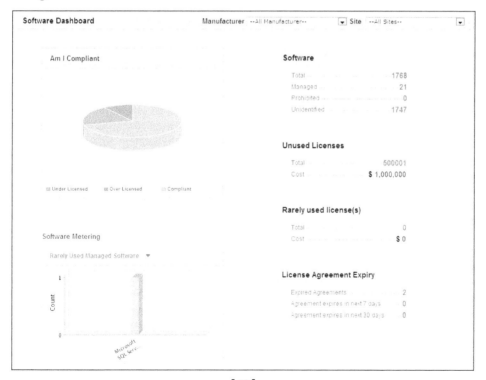

The **License Agreements** section can be used to keep track of and manage the end-user license agreements with the vendors.

The **Software Licenses** section comes in useful for managing specific software licenses:

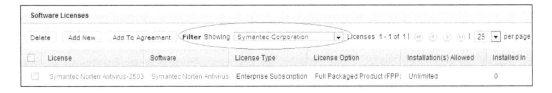

The **Service Packs** section tracks hotfixes, security updates, and other service packs released by the vendors:

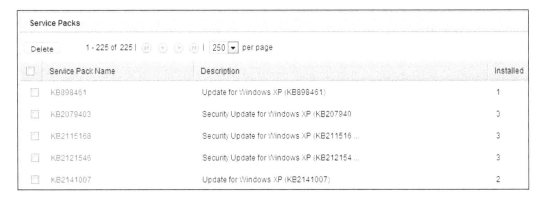

The **Groups** section helps to organize assets based on certain properties. For example, if there's often a requirement to find all workstations with less than 1 GB RAM, a dynamic group could be created for the same, as shown in the following screenshot:

Managing purchase orders

Now that we've seen the management of all types of assets and CIs in ServiceDesk Plus, we can focus on the only missing link of managing procurements and unassigned assets, or inventory. This can be done from the **Purchase** tab. The supplier's or vendor's information, along with the price quotes and offerings, can also be tracked under this module. The following screenshot represents the typical purchase order process flow:

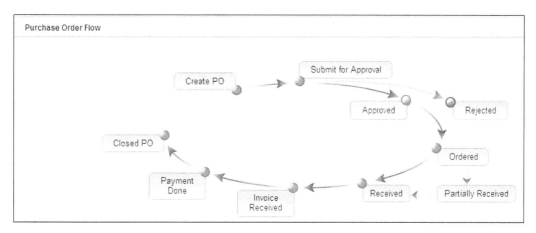

1. A new Purchase Order (PO) can be created by clicking on the **Create** PO button in the Purchase Order Flow block, or by clicking on the New Purchase Order button, or by choosing Purchase Order from the Create new section of the Quick Actions dropdown.

2. To approve or reject POs, the approver can click on the PO Name from the list of Purchase Orders and then click on Approve this PO or Reject this PO from the Actions dropdown on the tasks bar at the top. These options are visible only to the approvers of the purchase orders.

3. Once approved, the Actions | Order this PO option is used to order the items.

4. Once the item is received (fully or partially), the Receive items option is used to specify the quantity received.

 All the received items are automatically added as assets, except when the **Product Type** is **Consumable**. While this saves a lot of additional work, it might sometimes result in duplicates due to the automatic scan feature. In such cases, **Actions** | **Reconcile** can be used to remove such duplicates.

5. Similarly, the **Receive Invoice**, **Add Payment**, and **Payment Done** options can be used to add and track all received invoices and payments.

6. Once all the items and invoices are received, and payments done, the PO should be closed in the system from the **Close PO** button under the **Actions** tab.

Managing contracts

All assets need maintenance and organizations often have contracts with vendors for performing these maintenance activities from time to time. Similar to licenses, these contracts also have expiry periods and active management is required to keep the assets functioning to their best capacity, and at optimal cost. There can also be lease contracts, warranties, and other support contracts.

ServiceDesk Plus offers management of these contracts via the **Contracts** tab. A new contract can be created either from the **Quick Actions** dropdown, by clicking on the **Contract** button under the **Create new** section, or from the **New Contract** button within the **Contracts** page. There's also an option to import contracts from an XLS file using the **Import from XLS** button.

Contracts can also be marked as renewed from the **Actions | Renew Contract** option on the **Contract Details** page. It is recommended to give a new unique name to the renewed contract, instead of using the same as existing.

Summary

We've now seen the ways to manage assets (both IT and non-IT) via CMDB as CIs in ServiceDesk Plus, and now we are also aware of different methods and features for populating the CIs. We also now understand the concept of DML and how to manage its aspects as Software Assets. Finally, we delved into the capabilities of ServiceDesk Plus in managing purchase orders, inventories, and contracts. All of these together constitute IT Service Asset and Configuration Management (SACM).

Now that we can rely on an effective CMDB, it's a good time to start understanding how to manage changes in these CIs and how to put a control process in place effectively..

4

Controlling Changes and Releases

All changes or releases happen for one of two reasons:

1. Proactively seeking business benefits, such as offering new features to customers, reducing costs, improving the service, implementing compliance/audit/security/organizational guidelines, and so on.
2. Reactively resolving errors, bug fixes, and more.

A control process needs to be put in place to manage the risks associated with the changes and to effectively assess, optimize, and mitigate these risks, and all CIs must be put under this control process. A comprehensive Change Management System is required to support this process. In this chapter, we'll see how ServiceDesk Plus fits the bill and helps manage the change and release process flows. We'll cover the following topics in this chapter:

- Purpose, objective, and scope of Change Management and Release Management
- Process flow and Connection with IPM Process, as described in *Chapter 2, Managing Incidents and Problems*
- Role and responsibilities in Change and Release Management
- Risks and metrics to evaluate the success of Change and Release Management

There also needs to be a balance between the need for change against the impact of change, including the monetary aspects. Once the change implementation is agreed to be feasible, the Change and Release control mechanisms kick in with a defined set of steps to be followed. We'll dive into the process details, but let's start with the purpose, objective, and the scope of Change and Release Management processes. Please note that they are again two separate processes, but with a very close correlation.

Understanding the purpose, objective, and scope of Change and Release Management

Let us see the difference and the relationship between the two processes, while establishing their purpose, goals, objective, and scope.

The goal of the Change Management process is to respond to the business or IT requirements while maximizing value and reducing disruptions. The process ensures that:

- Standardized methods and procedures are used for all changes
- Changes to Assets and CIs are properly recorded in the assets DB and the CMDB
- Business risk is optimized

The objective of the **Change Management** process is to ensure that the changes are recorded, evaluated, authorized, prioritized, planned, tested, implemented, documented, and reviewed in a controlled manner.

The Change Management scope covers all service assets and CIs across the service life cycle. However, certain changes, like business operation changes, standard operational changes, and more, might be agreed to be put outside the Change Management control. These should be preidentified and communicated to the teams. The Change Management scope also covers any external service provider or component changes that might impact on the service delivery.

The goal of **Release Management** process is to deploy releases effectively, in order to deliver value to the customer and handover to service operations. The process ensures that:

- Release and deployment plans have been agreed with the stakeholders and customers
- The integrity of release packages is maintained and the same can be tracked, deployed, tested, verified, and backed out, if needed
- Users and support staff have the knowledge to use or support the service

The objective of Release Management is to ensure that change projects align to the established release and deployment plans and that the release packages are deployed efficiently and on schedule.

The release Management scope covers packaging, build, test, and deployment of release packages, and ensuring a smooth handover to service operations.

Effective Change and Release Management processes deliver changes safely and more quickly with optimal cost and risk and hence can make a significant difference to service costs and availability. We'll now see how to establish and have successful Change and Release Management processes using ServiceDesk Plus.

Understanding the process flow

Let us start with the implementation of the process.

Implementing the Change Management process flow

The Change Management process is very closely related to Configuration Management and Release Management, and hence the process model is designed in conjunction with them. It is important to understand and to differentiate between the types of changes. Broadly classifying, the changes could be of the following types:

- **Standard changes**: Preauthorized by Change Management, and has an accepted and established procedure with low risk. Many standard changes are triggered by service requests and directly actioned by the service desk. For example, password reset, standard application installation, and so on.

- **Normal changes**: All non-standard planned changes.

- **Emergency changes**: A change that must be implemented as soon as possible, for example, to resolve an incident.

The following diagram represents the process flow for a normal Request For Change (RFC) process:

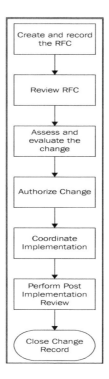

Step 1 – creating and recording the RFC

Changes can be requested by business units (for example, enhancements, business benefits, and more) or by the Problem Management staff (for example, error resolution, bug fixing, and more). An RFC should ideally capture the following details:

- Unique identifier for the RFC
- Trigger for the change (work order number, problem record number, and more)
- Description of the change
- Reason for the change

- Effect of not implementing the change
- CIs/baselines to be changed

 Baseline is a snapshot that is used as a reference point. It could also be the last known good configuration for certain changes.

- Details of the person/team proposing the change
- Proposed, scheduled, and actual date and time for the change
- Change category (significant, major, minor, or else)
- Predicted timeframe, resources, costs, and quality of service
- Proposed priority with justifications
- Risk assessments and mitigation plans
- Testing details and results, including sign-offs
- Back out / remediation plans
- Impact assessment
- Change decision body
- Authorizations
- Details of change implementers
- Change implementation results and reviews (success/failure, review details)

In ServiceDesk Plus, a new RFC can be created either from **Quick Actions | Change** under the **Create new** section *or* from the **New Change** button under the **Changes** tab. The following screenshot illustrates what the **New Change** form looks like:

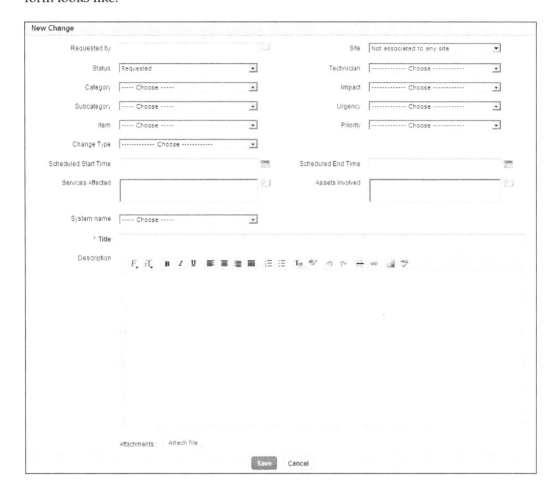

ServiceDesk Plus allows classification of changes into **Major**, **Minor**, **Significant**, and **Standard**, as shown in the dropdown in the following screenshot:

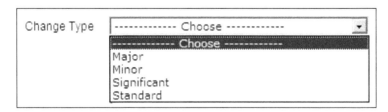

- **Standard change**: These are preapproved changes, as seen previously.

- **Minor change**: These are low-impact changes with minimum resource requirements. The Change Manager alone can approve such changes.

- **Major and significant changes**: These changes require approval from both the Change Manager and the identified Change Advisory Board (CAB).

 At the time of writing this book, an emergency change template was not offered in ServiceDesk Plus. This is planned in a future release with no tentative release date. However, a new Change Type can be configured from **Admin | Change Types** under the **Problem/Change management** block, as shown in the following screenshot:

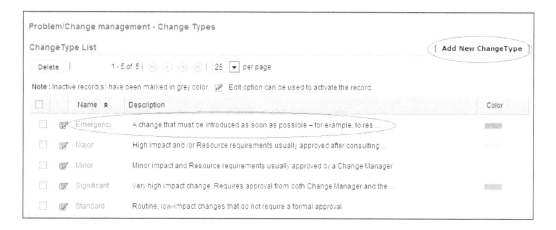

If the change is required due to an open problem, the relevant problem record should be associated with the change record. This can be done from the **Problems** tab within the Change window:

Special care should be taken while associating the impacted assets with the change, as this record will be used in updating the CMDB.

Step 2 – reviewing the RFC

A review process helps in eliminating change records which are impractical, incomplete, or duplicates. A senior team member, change manager, or the CAB might perform an initial quality review and approve or reject the change accordingly. In case of rejections due to the lack of details, the same change record could be updated and resubmitted.

Step 3 – assessing and evaluating the change

An overall view then needs to be taken in order to assess fully the impact of the change on services and assets. The different aspects of evaluating this impact together with the associated risks and benefits are clubbed under something known as the **seven Rs of Change Management**:

1. Who RAISED the change?
2. What is the REASON for the change?
3. What is the RETURN required from the change?
4. What are the RISKS involved in the change?
5. What RESOURCES are required to perform the change?
6. Who is RESPONSIBLE for the build, test, and implementation of the change?
7. What is the RELATIONSHIP between this change and other changes?

This assessment and evaluation is generally done by the Change Manager together with the CAB. CAB members may be preconfigured in ServiceDesk Plus. To create new CAB members, navigate to **Admin | Problem/Change management | Change Advisory Board(CAB)** and click on the **New CAB** button:

The New Change form itself could be customized to record the fields useful for the evaluation. Following are the steps to add a couple of fields to the **New Change** form for better Risk Assessment:

1. Go to **Admin | Change - Additional Fields** under the **Problem/Change management** block.

2. Configure two new fields under the **Text** tab as shown in the following, and **Save**:

3. Once saved, the new fields can be found under the **New Change** form:

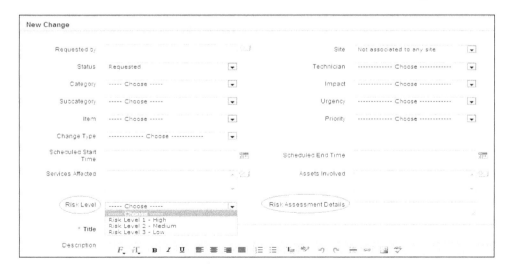

Another feature useful in helping to assess the conflicts, and hence the impact, is the **Calendar View**, located under the **Changes** tab, which can also be used for forward scheduling of changes. There are several preconfigured reports available in the **Reports** tab, which gives us a holistic view of all the pending changes:

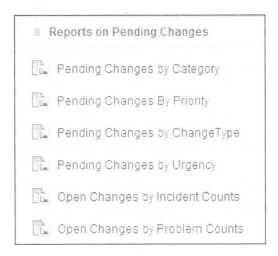

Step 4 – authorizing changes

Depending on the type and category of changes, an appropriate CAB and additional approvers might be chosen to authorize the change. These approvers are added from the **Approvals** tab in the Change window. Added CAB members can approve/reject the change using the appropriate button:

Step 5 – coordinating implementation

Authorized changes come to the Release Management staff for implementation. A change could require the involvement of various teams in its implementation, and coordination between them becomes vital. Similarly, it should be ensured that the change is being implemented within the scheduled window with the least amount of service disruption.

An overall **Roll Out Plan** and **Backout plan** can be added in the **Planning** tab of the Change window. Tasks can be assigned to various functions from the **Implementation** tab. Automated **Reminder** could be set and **Note** can be added by technicians from the **Add New** dropdown to aid in seamless coordination of the change implementation.

Any work log previously entered is visible under the **Work Log Details** section, or else a new entry could also be made by clicking on the "**Add New**" link. Similarly, any **Associated Project** can also be viewed or a new project could be associated with the change by clicking on the **Associate a project** link.

The Actual Release Management process flow is briefly discussed in the following section, *Implementing the Release Management Process Flow*.

Step 6 – performing a post-implementation review

Once the change is implemented successfully, it should be submitted back to the Change Management for a complete evaluation, and finally presented to the stakeholders for an agreement of acceptance, and closing any associated incidents, problems, and Known Error records.

If the change itself has resulted in an incident, a detailed review for the root cause is also done at this stage and any process improvements identified. Any revision in SLAs, OLAs, or contracts should also be considered in the same light.

The post-implementation review details can be entered under the **Review** tab.

Step 7 – closing the Change Record

Once the change is found to be complete in all respects, the record should be marked as closed by selecting the **Close Change** option from the **Actions** dropdown.

The complete history of the change record is available for audit or review purposes from the **History** tab in the Change window:

Implementing the Release Management process flow

The Release Management process is very closely related to the Change Management process and is often the technical side of it. However, it is important to note the process steps falling under the Release Management ambit, to ensure that releases and deployments are carefully and successfully executed. There are several approaches to deployments. It could be done either in a **Bing Bang approach** (that is, deployed to all users in one operation) or a **Phased approach** (that is, deployment in parts). It could follow either a **Push approach** (center pushing the deployment package to targets) or a **Pull approach** (users pulling the package at their own convenience). The deployment could also be done in an automated or a manual way.

Irrespective of the deployment methodology, an agreed and established process needs to be followed to ensure success and efficiency. A quick overview of the Release Management process is mentioned in the following steps:

 We'll not go into the details, considering it to be more of the technical side of things, and well covered within Change Management from process and service desk perspective.

Step 1 – planning the release

- Choosing the release model and approach
- Defining pass/fail criteria
- Finalizing build and test plans
- Planning pilots
- Planning the release packaging
- Deployment planning
- Logistics and delivery planning
- Financial planning

Step 2 – preparing for build, test, and deployment

- Verifying the service design and release design against the requirements
- Risk evaluation
- Documenting the predicted output
- Identifying people/teams for execution
- Identifying training needs and a training plan

Step 3 – building and testing

- Creating baseline and versions
- Managing test environments
- Executing test cases on CIs and components and recording results
- Controlling access rights
- Release packaging

Step 4 – testing service and pilots

- Integration testing
- Readiness (of service desk) testing
- Performing service rehearsals
- Piloting the release

Step 5 – preparing for deployment

- Finalizing implementation plan or the runbook
- Finalizing risk-mitigation plans
- Completing knowledge transfer or training sessions
- Making announcements/communications
- Making changes in continuity plans, if needed
- Mobilizing resources

Step 6 – performing deployment

- Transfer/Transition CIs, assets, components, and/or the service
- Decommission, remove, or retire the identified components

Step 7 – verifying

- Verifying the deployment
- Updating documentations
- Establishing measurements and reporting systems
- Gathering feedback
- Reporting and handling of any incidents due to the release

Step 8 – offering early-life support

- Resolve operational issues during an initial period after deployment
- Remove remaining errors or deficiencies

Step 9 – reviewing and closing the record

- Verifying activity logs and CMS contents

Establishing the roles and responsibilities of the service desk

The service desk might play the role of the coordinator of the Change and Release Management processes and is also the crucial link with Incident and Problem Management. However, even in cases of dedicated functions for these processes, certain responsibilities lie with the service desk:

- **Role of change initiator**: As part of Problem Management, the service desk may initiate changes required for problem resolution. Even for proactive changes, the service desk may log the change in the system and control its flow. The service desk may also raise change requests based on service requests.

- **Incident or Problem Manager**: Once the change is agreed to have been successfully resolved in the initial incident, the associated incidents and/or problem records are also marked as closed by the service desk. The service desk also raises any incident resulting from the change itself.

- **CAB Member**: The service desk should be represented on the Change Advisory Board as well.

- **Communicator**: All user communication, including details of the change schedules, projected service outage, and so on, is done by the service desk.

- **Knowledge Recipient**: The service desk receives the handovers and required training associated with the change in services, and changes should not be closed until this has occurred. It may even be appropriate to not approve the change until the handover and training plan is agreed.

- **Pilot**: The service desk is also an ideal function to participate in the pilot of the release, and to provide useful feedback as well as the sign-off for the release testing.

- **Implementer**: At certain times, the service desk is assigned a part of (or full) release deployment, especially for steps where only the service desk has authorized access *or* during emergency releases.

Assessing risks and identifying metrics

While the Change Management process itself is established to better understand and deal with risks, there are some risks inherent in the process implementation itself. The following should be kept in mind and addressed before starting to enforce the Change and Release Management processes:

- The additional layer might delay the delivery of critical changes and might be viewed as red tape, if it is not managed as part of an organizational Change Management process. People need to have it explained, convinced, and trained before any new process is mandated.

- The lack of a system supporting the organization's change process may impact the efficient delivery of the objective.

- If a clear distinction between operational, standard, and other changes is not established, the process might be overwhelmed and lose focus on more important changes.

- In case of a lack of audit or access control, the change process might be bypassed, putting significant risk to the services.

- Training and knowledge transition might not suffice if the business groups are not involved.

- In case of dependency on external vendors, there is less control, and hence an additional risk of missing the schedules.

- Missing relationships in the CMDB and compromise the impact assessment.

- Approval notifications could be missed or left without any action, holding up the releases. This could also happen when the approver is not available and the delegation is not set.

Measures should be aligned to business goals to help assess the performance of the Change and Release Management processes. Some suggested key performance indicators are:

- Number of changes meeting service requirements
- Cost versus benefit of changes
- Reduction in number of incidents
- Number of unauthorized changes
- Number of pending change requests
- Number of emergency changes
- Number of changes resulting in incidents
- Number of rejected changes
- Frequency of changes (categorized on CI types, and so on)
- Customer satisfaction index
- Deviation in change schedules

 There are several reports preconfigured in ServiceDesk Plus to keep track of the earlier mentioned indicators and more can easily be configured.

Summary

We now understand the extent of Change and Release Management with a detailed view of the process flow, and the ways in which it can be implemented in ServiceDesk Plus. We've also seen the risks and the KPIs to help with the continuous improvement of the processes.

After a thorough understanding of the critical processes of Incident Management, Problem Management, Configuration Management, Change Management, and Release Management, we are now well placed to dig deeper into the function of the Helpdesk and see how it envelops and completes the entire picture.

5
Service Desk – Where the Value Is Realized

While we've now seen some of the most important processes in IT Service Management, we haven't encountered any functions until now. We discussed the difference between a process and a function in *Chapter 1, Conceptualizing IT Service Management*, and now we're at the right juncture to see the first and the most important function within the ITSM Helpdesk.

Obviously, processes alone cannot deliver effective service operations. A stable infrastructure and skilled people are equally important for achieving this. These groups of people utilize the capability of the infrastructure to execute the defined processes, in order to help deliver value to the business.

In this chapter, we'll see why the Service Desk (or Helpdesk) lies at the core of IT Service Management and how this function could be used to control the critical processes.

Topics covered in this chapter are:

- **Service desk**: The visible face of the business
- Critical roles and responsibilities (such as Event Management, Incident Management, and so on)
- Value-adding responsibilities (Knowledge Management, reporting, backups, and so on)
- Challenges, critical success factors, and risks

However, before starting, we'll briefly discuss Service Operations and some of its other functions as well. These functions, together with the service desk and the processes provide the framework for the overall IT support structure.

The purpose of Service Operations is to coordinate and carry out the day-to-day activities and processes in order to deliver and manage services at the agreed level. This includes the execution and management of services, processes, technologies, and even the people.

- **Technical Management**: This function provides the technical skills and resources to support the operations. They can be developed into specialists in specific technologies to contribute in design, development, testing, release, and improvement of services.

- **Operations Management**: This function executes the day-to-day operational activities and consists of two functions in itself, which are:

  - ○ **Operations Control**: This function consists of operators of routine tasks. It also provides a central monitoring and control center.

  - ○ **Facilities Management**: Staffed by people responsible for management of the physical IT environment. For example, data centers, AC controls, server/computer rooms, and more.

- **Application Management**: This function is responsible for managing applications throughout their life cycle. This function is specialized in applications used to deliver day-to-day operational activities and hence contributes to the design, development, testing, release, and improvement of the same.

It should be noted that these functions execute the daily activities with a focus on optimizing the cost and quality of the services provided. They therefore play an important role in enabling the organization to meet its objectives. There needs to be a fine sense of balance to execute the day-to-day aspects effectively, while having a long-term perspective. Balance also needs to be maintained between certain other conflicting views, as illustrated in the following figure:

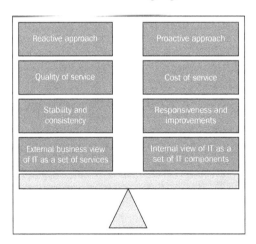

Service desk – the visible face of the business

A service desk is a functional unit made up of people responsible for dealing with a variety of service events.

While all the processes provide value to the business, the operational side is where the execution of the business is carried out and where the value is measured. This is the most visible side of the business. Additionally, it's the service desk which is the primary, and often the single, point of contact for the users, and hence, users perceive the organization from their experience with the service desk. The service desk also acts as the bridge between the users and the internal IT view. Even for cases where Technical or Application Management staff assistance is required, the service desk is generally the first point of contact for the users. The service desk can, hence, both compensate for the deficiencies, or vice versa, by creating a poor impression of an otherwise effective organization. That is why it's so important to get this function right.

The service desk is not only the best approach for dealing with the first line of IT support issues, but it also plays a vital role in improving customer service, satisfaction, and perception. By having the service desk as a single point of contact, accessibility of information and delivery of communication becomes much easier. This also helps the organization focus on service provision. Usage and productivity of resources is also made more efficient by having a single point of contact as a visible service desk. Often, the service desk is used as a learning ground to understand service management; however, care should be taken to avoid a reduction in the quality of support due to a lack of understanding of business knowledge.

The primary aim of the service desk is to restore *normal service* as quickly as possible. ITIL defines this normal service in the widest possible sense and could include fixing issues, fulfilling service requests, or simply answering queries.

The desk could be organized in any of the following structures, or any combination of these:

- **Local service desk**: This structure is in physical proximity to the users
- **Centralized service desk**: This structure is controlled from a single or comparatively smaller number of locations
- **Virtual service desk**: This is an impression of a centralized desk, through the use of technology
- **Follow-the-sun**: One of the most popular and widely followed models, which involves dispersing the staff at various geographical locations in order to provide round the clock coverage
- **Specialized groups**: These are specialist groups which handle requests related to their own area of expertize

Establishing the critical roles and responsibilities

The service desk, as we've seen, serves as the single point of contact for the users and has the primary responsibility of restoring normal service to users, to allow them to return to their work satisfactorily. There are several day-to-day tasks that help to achieve this objective, and which are the responsibility of the service desk:

- Logging and categorization of incidents and service requests
- Performing the first level of diagnosis and resolving incidents/requests they are capable of, and correctly and timely escalating the others
- Timely user communication and updates
- Closing incidents, requests, and others
- Conducting satisfaction surveys
- Updating the CMS

The service desk executes several processes and performs various roles in its day-to-day activities.

Managing events

This is the process to monitor all the events that occur throughout the IT infrastructure and to detect, manage, and escalate alerts and exceptions.

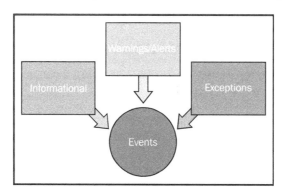

Events: A change of state that has significance for the management of IT service or a CI. They may be of the following three types:

Informational: Status or regular information of a CI, service, or an activity; often requires no further action.

Warnings/Alerts: Event of a CI or a service approaching a threshold. An action could be taken to avoid an exception.

Exception: Event signifying deviation in service level beyond the agreed tolerance levels.

The service desk is often assigned the responsibility for detecting and decoding events, and taking appropriate action. With its capability to monitor and report events, the service desk also forms the basis of continuous service improvement. If a service fails to meet the agreed targets, then it is considered to be **breaching** the SLA. With this role, the service desk also facilitates early detection of incidents, thus preventing such SLA breaches.

Raising event notifications

Notifications could be raised either due to approaching thresholds or via polling. ServiceDesk Plus offers features to make these notifications more meaningful and targeted to the right audience. Here are the steps to enable notification rules for purchases or contracts:

1. Navigate to **Admin | Purchase/ContractManagement** block, and then click on the **Notification Rules** option.

2. Select the relevant notification rules, and click on **Save**, as in the following screenshot:

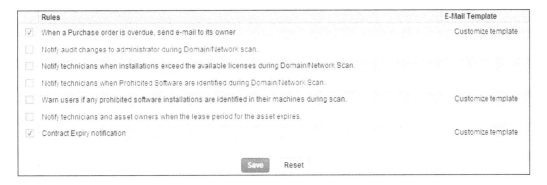

Here are the steps to configure notification rules for requests, problems, changes, solutions, tasks, and projects:

1. Navigate to **Admin | Helpdesk** block, and then click on the **Notification Rules** option.

2. Select the appropriate e-mail format.

3. Choose the appropriate tabs from the **Notification Rules** block, and select the relevant notifications.

4. Customize the e-mail templates from the **E-mail Templates for :** block, if needed.

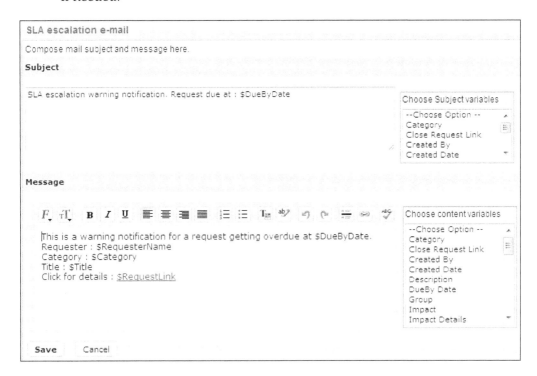

5. **Save** the record.

Comparing event correlations

Significant events are compared against a set of predefined rules to determine the business impact and take quick but effective action. These rules are called **Business Rules**. A correlation engine can be preprogrammed in ServiceDesk Plus to compare these events in a prescribed order. Here are the steps to do this:

1. Navigate to **Admin | Helpdesk** block, and click on the **Business Rules** option.

2. Click on the **Add New Business Rule** button at the top-right corner.

3. Fill in the details, as per the requirements, as illustrated in the following screenshot:

4. Click on **Save**.

5. The following items can be configured from the **Actions** dropdown:

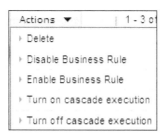

6. To change the order of execution, click on the **Organize Business Rules** button at the top right of the **Business Rules List** block.

Managing incidents

We've already seen the details of this process and the responsibilities of the service desk in its execution in *Chapter 2, Managing Incidents and Problems*. Now let's see, how the incident cost is calculated in ServiceDesk Plus, in the following steps:

1. Open the incident concerned from the **Requests** tab.
2. Choose **Add Work Log** from the **Actions** dropdown.
3. Select the technician from the **Owner** dropdown.
4. Select the **Start Time** and **End Time** of the work for the particular technician *or* enter the **Time Taken To Resolve**.
5. Enter any other charges incurred due to the incident in the **Other Charge** field.
6. The technician's cost is fetched and the cost fields are automatically calculated and populated.

Sometimes, due to multiple modes of communication or due to multiple users reporting the same issue, duplicate incidents can be logged into the system. ServiceDesk Plus allows the merging of these requests for proper controls and reporting:

In such cases, the oldest request is automatically treated as the parent request, and the subsequent ones are attached as conversational threads to the parent.

ServiceDesk Plus also lets us capture additional details, apart from the ones present in the incident form. This can be done from the:

1. **Admin | Helpdesk Customizer** option, under the **Helpdesk** block.

2. Click on **Incident – Additional Fields** from the left menu.

3. Choose the appropriate tab — **Text/Numeric/Date/Time/Decimal** — and fill in the required **Label** and other details.

4. Click on **Save**.

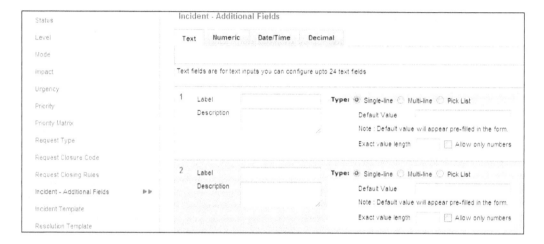

Managing problems

We've also seen the details of Problem Management and service desk responsibilities in *Chapter 2, Managing Incidents and Problems*. The problem cost could also be calculated in similar ways as discussed earlier for the incident cost.

The service desk also ensures, as part of the Problem Management responsibilities, that the incidents are not closed too early without full resolution. This puts an effective control in place and avoids reoccurrence of similar incidents. The service desk also plays an important role when the number of such open incidents keeps on increasing and posing the risk of becoming unmanageable. A purging strategy is then developed and acted upon with the assistance of the service desk.

Fulfilling service requests

Often, the majority of the requests received by the service desk are requests for information, minor assistance, and standard changes. Such requests are called **service requests**, and their life cycle is managed under the Request Fulfillment process. Some organizations may choose to implement this within the Incident Management process by defining a specific category in Incident Management for service requests. Here are the steps to combine service requests with incidents:

1. Navigate to **Admin | General** block and click on **Self-Service Portal Settings**.
2. Scroll down to the **Request Feature List**.
3. **Enable Combine incident and service templates listing for the service**.
4. Click on **Save**.

ServiceDesk Plus does not enforce either approach and could be used with equal ease in both cases. It handles both incidents and service requests under the **Requests** tab. If the incidents and service requests are *not* combined, an additional dropdown, **Service Catalog** is also shown at the top bar, which can be used for raising service requests:

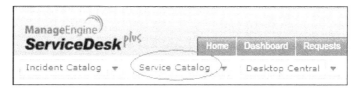

The subcategories of services and specific services under these categories can be managed from **Admin | Service Catalog** option under the **Helpdesk** block:

ServiceDesk Plus also allows the editing and closing of multiple requests together. Mandatory fields and notifications can also be configured as per request closure rules.

As we've previously seen, incident and problem costs can be calculated using the time given by the resources. However, many times, the requests are put on wait for response from other teams/people, or for other reasons. In such circumstances, the timer needs to be put on hold for correct calculations and to avoid false breaches. There are two important settings in ServiceDesk Plus that should be be noted for this purpose:

1. **Automatic stopping/starting the timer in certain conditions**: To configure the agreed action, navigate to **Admin | General | Self-Service Portal Settings | Request Feature List**.

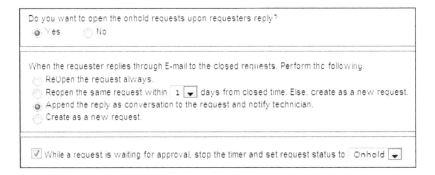

2. **Manual stopping/starting the timer**: The status of the request could be set to On Hold, when the timer is to be stopped. Once this is set, an option is shown in the **Actions** dropdown, in the request details page, to start the timer again:

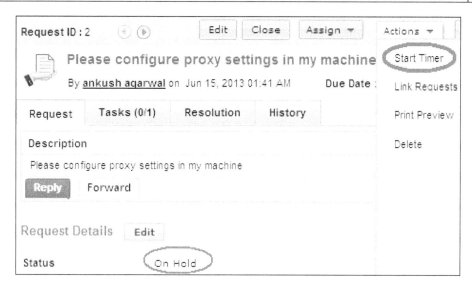

 Request statuses can be customized from **Admin | Helpdesk | Helpdesk Customizer | Status**.

Managing access

Service desk also plays a significant role in this process of managing the security triad of confidentiality, integrity, and availability. Being the first point of contact for users, it is imperative for the service desk to establish the identity of the requestor before making the authorized services available to them.

Here are some of the important options available in ServiceDesk Plus to control this triad. All of the following options can be accessed from the **Admin** tab:

- **Mail server settings**: This enables password controlled accesses, SPAM filtering, and more
- **Regions, sites**, and **departments**: These options are for controlling local/regional/departmental accesses
- User roles
- Requestors and technicians
- Support groups and user groups
- Active directory and LDAP features

Other processes

Apart from the operational processes discussed earlier, the service desk also participates in several other processes:

- Change and Release Management
- Configuration Management
- Capacity and Availability Management
- Financial Management
- Service Continuity Management

Understanding the value-adding responsibilities

Now that we've seen the critical responsibilities of the service desk, let's also discuss some of the most common value-adding activities that the service desk conducts:

Understanding Knowledge Management

The value of collecting and churning data to turn it into information, knowledge, and finally, wisdom, is well known across organizations. The service desk, being situated at the core of IT Service Management, is often considered the function best placed to collect data and maintain a Knowledge Management System. The service desk is also the first in line for event monitoring, and hence best placed to spot trends and to help prioritize the actions.

One of the most important modules in ServiceDesk Plus to assist in Knowledge Management, is the **Solutions** tab. This allows the service desk to record solutions for future reference:

The solutions are stored in a parent-child tree-like structure and can be managed from the **Manage Topics** link. Some of the other important options are also highlighted in the earlier screenshot.

- **Browse by Topics**: This dropdown lets you choose any of the available topics for viewing or editing.

- **New Solution**: As the name suggests, this button can be used to create a new solution.

- **All Solutions**: This is the dropdown to filter and show only the approved solutions / approval pending solutions / unapproved solutions / rejected solutions. The default setting is to show all solutions.

Solutions which have been sent for approval, but have not yet been approved/rejected, are shown under **Approval Pending Solutions**. Solutions, which are yet to be sent for approval, are shown under **Unapproved Solutions**.

Manage Topics				
Available Topics			Add New Topic	
Topic name	**Solutions**		**Actions**	
• General	0	Rename	Change Parent	Delete
• Hardware	0	Rename	Change Parent	Delete
• Desktop Hardware	0	Rename	Change Parent	Delete
• Printers	0	Rename	Change Parent	Delete
• New Models	0	Rename	Change Parent	Delete
• Printer Type A	0	Rename	Change Parent	Delete
• Printer Type B	0	Rename	Change Parent	Delete
• Older Models	0	Rename	Change Parent	Delete

Generating reports

The output of the monitoring activity needs to be collated, analyzed, and distributed to management and stakeholders for their consumption. Once the critical success factors (CSF), KPIs, metrics, and corresponding action plans have been defined, regular quantitative assessment reports need to be produced and distributed to the decision makers in order to address issues and to help improve the services. ServiceDesk Plus offers the following types of reports to help achieve this:

Using predefined ServiceDesk Plus reports

There are several reports predefined in ServiceDesk Plus to monitor the following areas:

- **Helpdesk reports**: These are reports on incidents, service requests, SLAs, and so on.

- **Problem/Change reports**: These are reports on pending/completed problems or changes.

- **Time/cost reports**: These are, for example, reports on time spent, cost, and so on by technicians. These reports can be grouped under various categories.

- **Survey reports**: These are reports on various surveys, as shown in the following screenshot:

- **Asset reports**: These include various workstation, server, software, and other asset-related metrics.

- **Audit reports**: These include reports on audit history by workstation, by timeline, and by changes.

- **Resources reports**: These include reports on resources by product types, vendors, and by site.

- **Contract reports**: These reports are on active contracts, max values, by status, by vendors, and so on.

- **Purchase reports**: These are reports on purchases, and are similar to contract reports.

Using custom reports

ServiceDesk Plus also offers the ability to create custom reports based on certain requirements, as shown in the following screenshot:

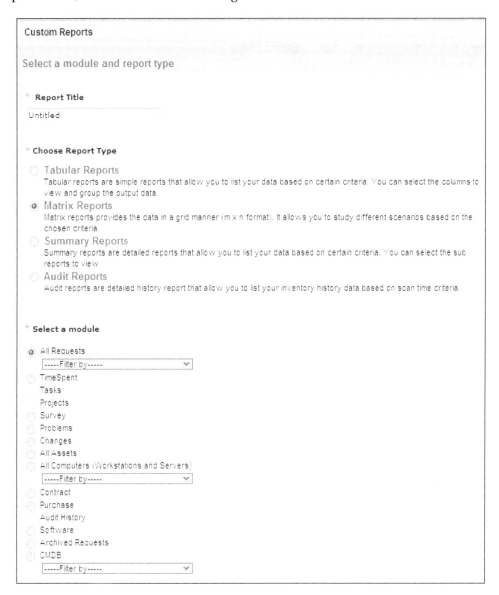

Using query reports

ServiceDesk Plus also lets us run database queries to further control the data extraction and rows/columns to be included in our reports. The **Frequently Asked Reports** is a very useful button, not only to generate reports quickly, but also to get an idea of the queries ServiceDesk Plus executes. The help card can also be referred to for some quick and useful tips.

The following screenshot is the table schema of the ServiceDesk Plus database, which can be referred for editing queries:

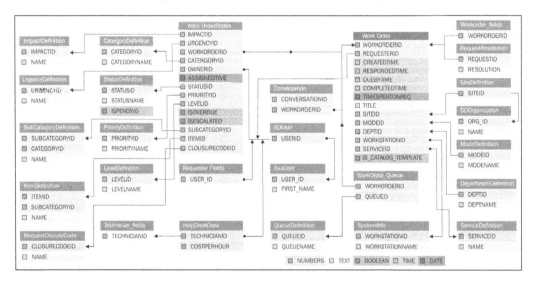

Using flash reports

Flash reports are used to get a quick and customizable view of various reports based on created time, due by time, and so on. Here is a screenshot of a sample report:

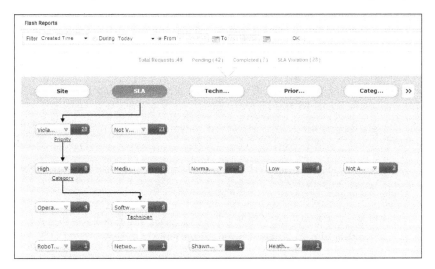

Using scheduled reports

These are the automated reports, which could be generated and e-mailed once, daily, weekly, or monthly:

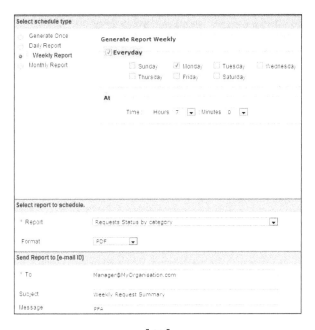

Managing the administrative and housekeeping tasks

The service desk is often assigned several administrative and housekeeping tasks. Some of the most common ones are as follows:

- **Central coordination point**: These tasks consist of managing various processes, executing routine operational activities, and reporting

- **Operations bridge**: This task consists of acting as a link between the operations teams and the IT technology and application teams

- **Job scheduling**: This task consists of managing various routine activities, housekeeping, and reports

- **Backup and restore**: This task consists of managing and executing the continuity plans

 To backup ServideDesk Plus data navigate to **Start | All Programs | ManageEngine ServiceDesk Plus | Backup Data**

or go to the `backUpData.bat` file within the `<ServiceDesk>\ bin` folder. This can be used for backing up ServiceDesk Plus data. `restoreData.bat` file can be used for restoring this backup.

Understanding the challenges, critical success factors, and risks

There are several challenges and risks associated with the service desk function. Also, it being the user-facing side of IT, it is extremely critical to be aware of these challenges and have plans to manage the same.

Understanding the challenges

- Managing the ongoing cost of services

- Addressing design, testing, or deployment flaws, especially in the absence of additional funding

- Varying user expectations

- Filtering and managing the significant events

- The ability to identify and authorize requestors

- Engagement with technical and application teams

- Involvement with the management of other processes

Understanding the critical success factors

- Clearly defined SLAs, OLAs, and contracts
- Agreed and documented standard requests and authorization details
- Management support
- Business support
- Staffing and retention
- Validity of testing and quality assurance

Assessing risks

- Unavailability of training or resources
- Inadequate monitoring or reporting capabilities
- Change in authorization levels due to changes in teams, locations, and so on
- Service loss

Summary

We've now seen the importance of organizing the service desk to help the business and its customers. This chapter covered various critical and value-adding responsibilities of the service desk and ways in which to achieve them in ServiceDesk Plus. The need to balance between contrasting responsibilities was also discussed.

We've now covered the most important processes and features in ServiceDesk Plus and will see some of the handy features before closing in the next chapter.

6
Making Life Easier – Handy Features

Now that we've covered most of the critical processes and the ways to implement them in ServiceDesk Plus, it's time to see some of the miscellaneous features to help us in our day-to-day tasks. We'll be covering the following useful features in this chapter:

- Knowledge base
- Remote control
- E-mail commands
- Data archiving
- User survey

Revisiting the knowledge base

We've seen the importance of Knowledge Management and the management of a knowledge base in *Chapter 5*, *Service Desk – Where the Value is Realized*. The approved and published solutions can be accessed by all without even logging into ServiceDesk Plus by using the following link:

```
http://<server name>:<port number>/sd/SolutionsHome.sd
```

To redirect the URL to the relevant page you need to enter the `<server name>` (for example, `localhost`), and the port ServiceDesk Plus is running on (for example, `8080`). You can also navigate to the **Solutions** tab if you're already logged in.

To view the solutions which are still to be sent for approval (unapproved), or the solutions which have been sent but are pending approval, or the rejected solutions, we can use the **Filter Showing** dropdown in the **Solutions** block, as shown in the following screenshot:

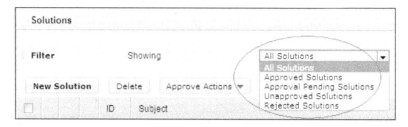

Using the remote control

With the remote control feature, ServiceDesk Plus allows us to access and control workstations (with the agreement of the end user) located far from the helpdesk. Only the technicians who have been assigned the role of **AERemoteControl** are allowed to perform remote control on workstations. The roles can be assigned by navigating to **Admin | Roles** under the **Users** block. The following screenshot illustrates the various roles in ServiceDesk Plus:

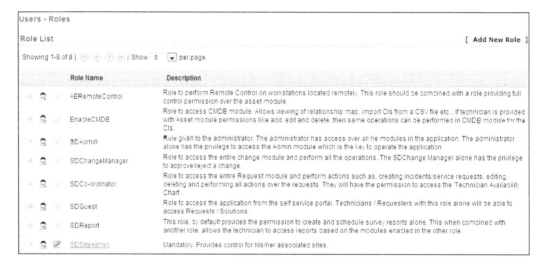

Remote control for all workstations can be enabled/
disabled by navigating to **Admin | Self-Service Portal
Settings** under the **General** block, and then selecting the
radio buttons from the **Remote Control Access** block.

To access a remote workstation, the following steps are to be performed:

1. Go to the **Assets** tab.
2. Click on **Workstation**, listed under **IT Assets** in the left-hand menu.
3. Find and click on the name of the workstation that is to be accessed.
4. Choose a method from the **Remote Control** dropdown in the **Tasks** bar
   at the top.

 If Agent.exe is not already installed, then it has to be
installed on the local drive and an ActiveX control has to
run as the viewer.

Controlling with e-mail commands

We've seen the setting of the business rules and how this can help in auto-assigning
the category and priority of tickets. However, to get a finer control and not let things
get too complicated, with hundreds of rules, the **E-mail Command** feature can be
used in ServiceDesk Plus. This also enables remote technicians and even third-
party support teams to update records without the need to have a license. It can be
configured using the following steps:

1. Navigate to **Admin | Mail Server Settings** under the **Helpdesk** block.
2. Click on the **E-mail Command** tab.
3. Check the **Enable E-mail Command** checkbox.
4. The **E-mail Subject contains** field is used to determine which e-mails have to
   be parsed. The string given here between the delimiters is the subject criteria
   for e-mails to be parsed. For example, if the value given is @Ticket@, then all
   e-mails with @Ticket@ would be parsed.
5. Any special character can be used as a delimiter and the same can be
   mentioned in the **Command Delimiter** field.

6. The **Sample e-mail content** field is also provided for reference. The **Help card** below can also be quickly referred to for configurable values.

Archiving data for housekeeping

With hundreds of requests and records being recorded almost on a daily basis, the performance of ServiceDesk Plus can easily degrade in the absence of proper housekeeping. Therefore, an archival plan is vital to keep the software performing at its best. The archived requests are stored separately from the active requests and have separate search and reporting options. However, it should be noted that the requests, once archived, cannot be modified, deleted, or moved back to the active state.

The following steps are taken to configure data archiving in ServiceDesk Plus:

1. Navigate to **Admin | Data Archiving** from under the **General** block.
2. Check the **Enable Scheduled Data Archiving** checkbox.
3. Set the required parameters as shown in the following screenshot:

 Once archived, the requests can be seen by navigating to **Requests | All Requests** dropdown, and then clicking on the **Archived Requests** option, or by navigating to **Quick Actions | Archived Requests**.

Conducting user surveys

A very interesting feature provided in ServiceDesk Plus is the ability to conduct customer satisfaction surveys and generate reports based on the same. Customized surveys with predefined frequency can easily be created in ServiceDesk Plus. Here are the steps to create customized surveys:

Go to **Admin | User Survey** block. The visible options in the block are described in the following:

- **Survey Settings**: The **Survey Settings** option allows us to enable/disable the survey by ticking the **Enable User Survey** checkbox, and also allows us to configure **Welcome Message, E-mail Content, Success Message, Failure Message, Thanks Message,** and to **Schedule Survey.**

- **Define Survey**: The **Define Survey** option lets us add questions, define satisfaction levels, and even translate the survey into different languages:

- **Survey Preview**: This option is not visible under the **Admin** tab, but available under the **User Survey** block in the left-hand menu. As the name suggests, the **Survey Preview** option provides a preview of the configured survey, before it is sent to the customer.

- **Survey Results**: Finally, **Survey Results** is the place where the feedback received can be seen.

Summary

This chapter covered some of the important features included in ServiceDesk Plus that help users with some of the small and important day-to-day tasks. The software also contains several other helpful features and the reader is encouraged to explore them as those are mostly self-explanatory and best experienced hands-on. These features enhance the overall experience of using the software.

This brings us to the end of the book and we sincerely hope that it has not only helped you in using ServiceDesk Plus pleasurably, but also in understanding the ITSM processes behind it and how those can be utilized to make the team and the organization more effective.

Index

CSV file
  using 38
Customer Based SLA 7
Customer facing services 9
custom reports
  using 81

D

data
  archiving, for housekeeping 90
Define Survey option 92
Definitive Media Library (DML) 42, 43

E

E-mail Command feature
  about 89
  configuring 89
events
  about 69
  correlations, comparing 71, 72
  managing 68
  notifications, changing 69-71
exception 69

F

Facilities Management 66
flash reports
  using 83
Follow-the-sun 67
FrequentlyAsked Reports 82
function
  and process, differentiating 7
Functional escalation 22

G

Groups section 44

H

Helpdesk reports 80
Hierarchical escalation 22
housekeeping
  data, archiving for 90
  tasks 84

I

Incident Management
  about 12
  issues 12
  metrics, before adapting 31
  process flow, implementing 14
  requisites 13, 14
  risks, before adapting 31
  scope 12
Incident Management process flow, imple-
      menting
  incidents, categorizing 18
  incidents, closing 23
  incidents, diagnosing 21
  incidents, escalating 22
  incidents, identifying 15-17
  incidents, logging 15, 16
  incidents, prioritizing 19, 20
  incidents, recovering from 23
  incidents, resolving 23
Incident
  categorizing 18
  closing 23
  diagnosing 21
  escalating 22
  identifying 16
  logging 15, 16
  managing 73, 74
  prioritizing 19, 20
  recovering 23
  resolving 23
informational 69
Information Model
  creating 40
IPM process flow. *See* Incident Manage-
      ment process flow, implementing
ITIL 5
IT Service Category 9
IT Service Management. *See* ITSM
ITSM 5, 6

K

knowledge base
  revisiting 87
Knowledge Management 78, 79
Known Error database (KEDB) 21, 28

L

License Agreements section 44
local service desk 67

M

Mail server
  settings 77
Manage dropdown
  additional fields 10
  SLAs 10
metrics
  before adapting Change management,
    identifying 63
  before adapting Incident management,
    identifying 31
  before adapting Problem management,
    identifying 31
Multilevel SLA 7

N

Network Scan 39
New Change form 57

O

OLA
  and SLA, differentiating 7, 8
Operational Level Agreement. *See* OLA
Operations Control 66
Operations Management 66

P

Phased approach 60
Proactive Problem Management 13
Problem/Change reports 80
Problem Management
  about 13
  processes 13
  requisites 13, 14
Problem Management, processes
  Proactive Problem Management 13
  Reactive Problem Management 13

Problem Management process flow,
    implementing
  about 25
  problem, detecting 26
  problem, categorizing 28
  problem, closing 29, 30
  problem, diagnosing 28, 29
  problem, investigating 28, 29
  problem, logging 27, 28
  problem, prioritizing 28
  problem, resolving 29
problems
  categorizing 28
  closing 29
  detecting 26
  diagnosing 28
  investigating 28
  logging 27
  prioritizing 28
  resolving 29
process
  and function, differentiating 6, 7
Pull approach 60
purchase orders
  managing 45, 46
Purchase reports 80
Push approach 60

Q

query reports
  using 82

R

Reactive Problem Management 13
Relationships 34
release
  planning 60
Release Management
  about 50
  goal 50
  key performance indicators 64
  objective 50
  scope 50

Thank you for buying
ServiceDesk Plus 8.x Essentials

About Packt Publishing

Packt, pronounced 'packed', published its first book "*Mastering phpMyAdmin for Effective MySQL Management*" in April 2004 and subsequently continued to specialize in publishing highly focused books on specific technologies and solutions.

Our books and publications share the experiences of your fellow IT professionals in adapting and customizing today's systems, applications, and frameworks. Our solution based books give you the knowledge and power to customize the software and technologies you're using to get the job done. Packt books are more specific and less general than the IT books you have seen in the past. Our unique business model allows us to bring you more focused information, giving you more of what you need to know, and less of what you don't.

Packt is a modern, yet unique publishing company, which focuses on producing quality, cutting-edge books for communities of developers, administrators, and newbies alike. For more information, please visit our website: www.packtpub.com.

Writing for Packt

We welcome all inquiries from people who are interested in authoring. Book proposals should be sent to author@packtpub.com. If your book idea is still at an early stage and you would like to discuss it first before writing a formal book proposal, contact us; one of our commissioning editors will get in touch with you.

We're not just looking for published authors; if you have strong technical skills but no writing experience, our experienced editors can help you develop a writing career, or simply get some additional reward for your expertise.

Microsoft Dynamics CRM 2011: Dashboards Cookbook

ISBN: 978-1-849684-40-8   Paperback: 266 pages

Over 50 simple but incredible effective recipes for creating, customizing, and interacting with rich dashboards and charts

1. Take advantage of all of the latest Dynamics CRM dashboard features for visualizing your most important data at a glance.

2. Understand how iFrames, chart customizations, advanced WebResources and more can improve your dashboards in Dynamics CRM by using this book and eBook.

3. A highly practical cookbook bursting with a range of exciting task-based recipes for mastering Microsoft Dynamics CRM 2011 Dashboards.

CiviCRM Cookbook

ISBN: 978-1-782160-44-1   Paperback: 236 pages

Master this web-based constituent relationship management software for nonprofit and civic sector organizations

1. Take your CiviCRM skills to the next level and harness the power of CiviCRM

2. Covers a wide range of CiviCRM core and component topics

3. Practical, comprehensive, in-depth and well-explained recipes with the necessary screenshots

Please check **www.PacktPub.com** for information on our titles

Force.com Tips and Tricks

ISBN: 978-1-849684-74-3   Paperback: 224 pages

A quick refrence guide for administrators and developers to get more products with Force.com

1. Tips and tricks for topics ranging from point-and-click administration, to fine development techniques with Apex & Visualforce

2. Avoids technical jargon, and expresses concepts in a clear and simple manner

3. A pocket guide for experienced Force.com developers

Microsoft Dynamics CRM 2011 Applications (MB2-868) Certification Guide

ISBN: 978-1-849686-50-1   Paperback: 344 pages

A practical guide on how to use and manage Microsoft Dynamics CRM 2011 that focuses on helping you to pass the Microsoft certification exam

1. Comprehensive step-by-step guide to help you prepare for the MB2-868 exam

2. Loaded with screenshots and key points to help you pass the certification exam

3. Sample a 75 question practice exam to test your knowledge before you participate in the real exam